ANTIPASTI!
Appetizers the Italian Way

ANTIPASTI!
Appetizers the Italian Way

Text by Carla Bardi
Photography by Marco Lanza
Set Design by Cinzia Calamai

TIME LIFE BOOKS

TIME-LIFE BOOKS IS A DIVISION OF TIME LIFE INC.

TIME-LIFE CUSTOM PUBLISHING

Vice President and Publisher   Terry Newell
Associate Publisher   Teresa Hartnett
Vice President of Sales and Marketing   Neil Levin
Director of New Product Development   Quentin McAndrew
Director of Special Sales   Liz Ziehl

TIME-LIFE is a trademark of Time Warner Inc. U.S.A.

Library of Congress Cataloging-in-Publication Data

Antipasti! : appetizers the Italian way / Carla Bardi
    p.   cm. -- (Pane & vino)
   Includes index.
   ISBN 0-7835-5269-6
    I. Appetizers. 2. Cookery, Italian.   I. Title. II. Series
TX740.C27 1998
641.8'12'0945--dc2I

97-26248
CIP

© McRae Books 1997

Conceived, edited and designed by McRae Books, Florence, Italy
Text: Carla Bardi
Photography: Marco Lanza
Set Design: Cinzia Calamai

Design: Marco Nardi
Translation from the Italian: Erika Paoli
Editing: Alison Leach, Lynn McRae and Anne McRae
Illustrations: Paola Holguín

The Publishers would like to thank Sbigoli (Florence), Mastrociliegia (Fiesole),
Pasquinucci (Florence), Sara Vignozzi, Alessandro Frassinelli and Leonardo Pasquinelli
for their assistance during the production of this book.

Color separations: Fotolito Toscana, Florence, Italy
Printed and bound in Italy by Grafiche Editoriali Padane, Cremona

Other titles in the same series:

Zuppe Risotti Polenta! Italian Soup, Rice and Polenta Dishes

Pastissima! Pasta the Italian Way

Verdure! Vegetables the Italian Way

CONTENTS

INTRODUCTION

In one of my favorite restaurants in Piedmont, in northern Italy, ordering an "antipasto misto" means succumbing to the delights of 8–10 tiny portions of vegetable, meat, and fish appetizers. Every morsel, served separately to each guest, is just sufficient to arouse appetites, never to satisfy them. Hardly have you savored one when your plate is whisked away and another appears. The dishes continue in a crescendo of taste, texture and color until, just as you begin to wonder whether the rest of the meal will be necessary, the dish of steaming pasta you forgot you had ordered arrives and the meal moves onto the next phase. The moral of the story is that when serving antipasti, always keep the portions small. You may, as I often do, prefer to serve a number of appetizers and skip the pasta course. In this case, increase the number of dishes, not their size. You will find over 100 suggestions for appetizers in this book, the gleanings of a lifetime from an antipasti addict. For your convenience, they have been organized into four chapters according to the main ingredients — Vegetable, Egg & Cheese, Fish, and Meat.

Herbs and Spices

These are a selection of the most common herbs and spices used to prepare Italian appetizers. Most of them will be familiar and readily available in fresh fruit and vegetable stores and markets. As a general rule, fresh herbs are better than dried, and dried herbs are better than powdered; whether powdered herbs are better than none is debatable!

MARJORAM

CLOVES

CHILIES

CHIVES

CILANTRO

GARLIC

PAPRIKA

ROSEMARY

SAFFRON

FENNEL SEEDS

THYME

BASIL

BAY LEAVES

HERBS

Many herbs are easy to grow, so if you have a garden, terrace, balcony or window-box, invest in some plants and you will always have a ready supply within easy reach.

DILL

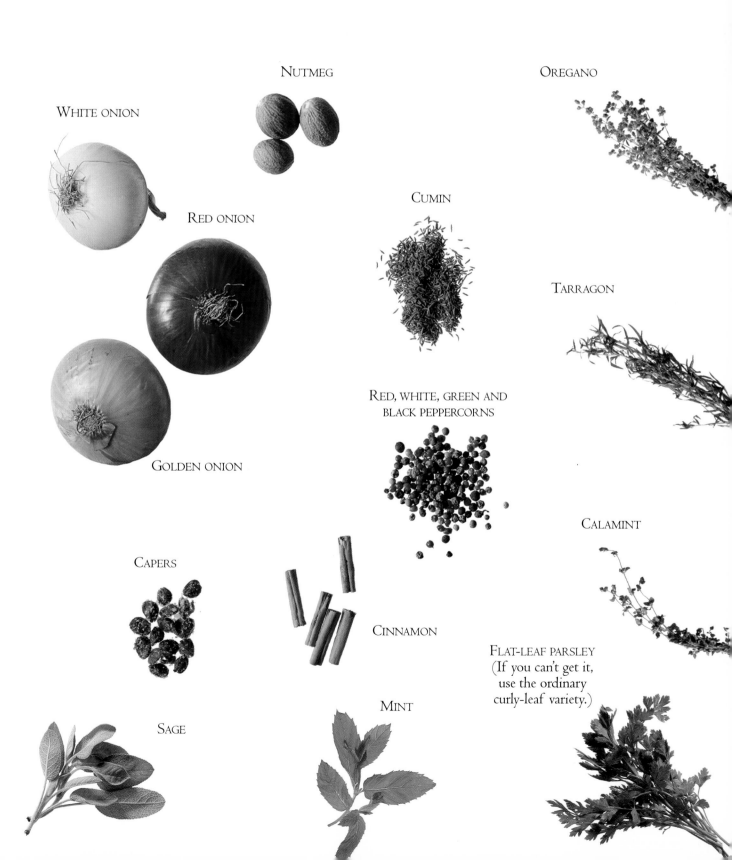

NUTMEG

OREGANO

WHITE ONION

CUMIN

RED ONION

TARRAGON

RED, WHITE, GREEN AND
BLACK PEPPERCORNS

GOLDEN ONION

CALAMINT

CAPERS

CINNAMON

FLAT-LEAF PARSLEY
(If you can't get it,
use the ordinary
curly-leaf variety.)

MINT

SAGE

Meats and Cheeses

Many of the recipes in this book make use of special Italian meats or cheeses. Because of the success that Italian cuisine now enjoys abroad, most are widely available outside Italy. However, as always, be flexible about ingredients; the descriptions here are designed not only to help you recognize them, but also to help you decide what local product could be used in their place.

Mortadella
The best mortadella comes from Bologna, in central Italy, where it was first made in about 1300. The special blend of beef, pork, and spices is steamed for many hours and then slowly dried.

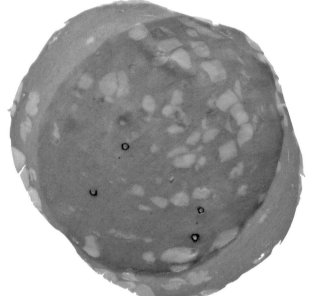

Prosciutto
Prosciutto is made throughout Italy, but the finest quality prosciutto comes from Parma, in the north. The raw ham is cured in salt and then aged for anywhere from between 9 months to 2 years.

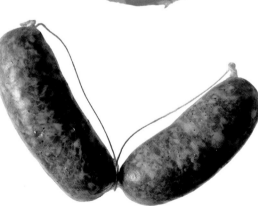

Ham
Ham is cured in salt and then slowly steam-cooked. Served by itself, or with potato salad (see p. 108), it makes a tasty appetizer. It is also used to flavor sauces and as toppings for fried polenta, *crostini*, and many other dishes.

Sausages
There are many different types of *salsicce* (Italian sausages). They are all made of fresh, raw meat and are usually flavored with herbs and spices. They are delicious when broiled or barbecued, but can also be fried, used to flavor dishes or eaten raw.

GRUYÈRE
This is a classic Swiss cheese. It is widely used in Italy, both for cooking and as a table cheese.

PECORINO GIOVANE
Pecorino giovane is a young sheep's cheese. Usually served as a table cheese, it is also very good in salads, particularly with broad beans, apples or celery.

PECORINO STAGIONATO
Pecorino stagionato is aged for at least a year. It is used both as a table cheese and to grate over and flavor many dishes.

EMMENTHAL
Another Swiss cheese widely used in Italian cuisine. Made of cow's milk, it is characterized by the large holes in its texture.

PROVOLONE
This cheese comes from southern Italy. Once produced with buffalo milk, it is now usually made of cow's milk. It is used both young and aged as a table cheese and for cooking.

PARMIGIANO
Parmesan cheese is made from cow's milk. It is aged for 2-3 years. It makes an excellent table cheese and is also good for flavoring all sorts of dishes, from pasta and risotto, to appetizers and vegetables.

GORGONZOLA
This cheese takes its name from a village in Lombardy, in northern Italy. A specially introduced mold is encouraged to grow during the aging process; this produces the blue veins and blotches and the distinctive tangy flavor in the creamy cow's milk base.

MOZZARELLA
A Neapolitan cheese once made with water buffalo's milk. Many good cow's milk varieties are now available.

MASCARPONE
This soft, creamy cheese also comes from Lombardy. Made of fresh cow's cream, it will only keep a day or two in the refrigerator.

CAPRINO
Caprino is made of goat milk. It is sold fresh or aged. The creamy, fresh caprino is used in many recipes for appetizers; the aged varieties can be served at table or included in salads and cooked dishes.

RICOTTA
Fresh ricotta has a delicious light and delicate flavor. It is made of goat, ewe's or cow's milk. Always try to buy it fresh and avoid the brands sold in plastic containers.

SEAFOOD AND OTHER INGREDIENTS

The simplicity of most *antipasto* dishes means that only the finest and freshest of ingredients should be used. Most of the fish-based appetizers will be best if prepared with fresh seafood from the market.

WALNUTS

PINE NUTS

RAISINS

ALMONDS

BLACK OLIVES

GREEN OLIVES

CAESAR'S MUSHROOMS
(ROYAL AGARIC)

PORCINI
MUSHROOMS

WHITE
MUSHROOMS

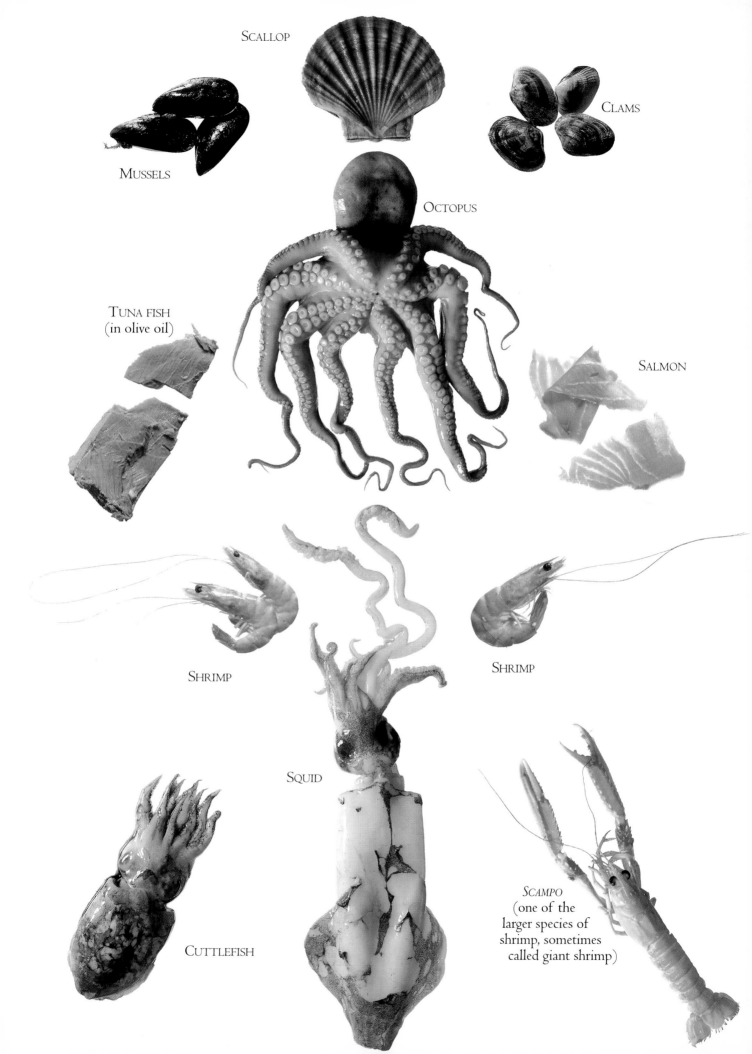

SCALLOP

CLAMS

MUSSELS

OCTOPUS

TUNA FISH
(in olive oil)

SALMON

SHRIMP

SHRIMP

SQUID

CUTTLEFISH

SCAMPO
(one of the
larger species of
shrimp, sometimes
called giant shrimp)

UTENSILS

Preparing delicious *antipasti* does not require unusual or special kitchen equipment. If you don't already own one, a grill pan may be a good addition to your kitchenware. This is a selection of the cookware used to make the recipes in this collection.

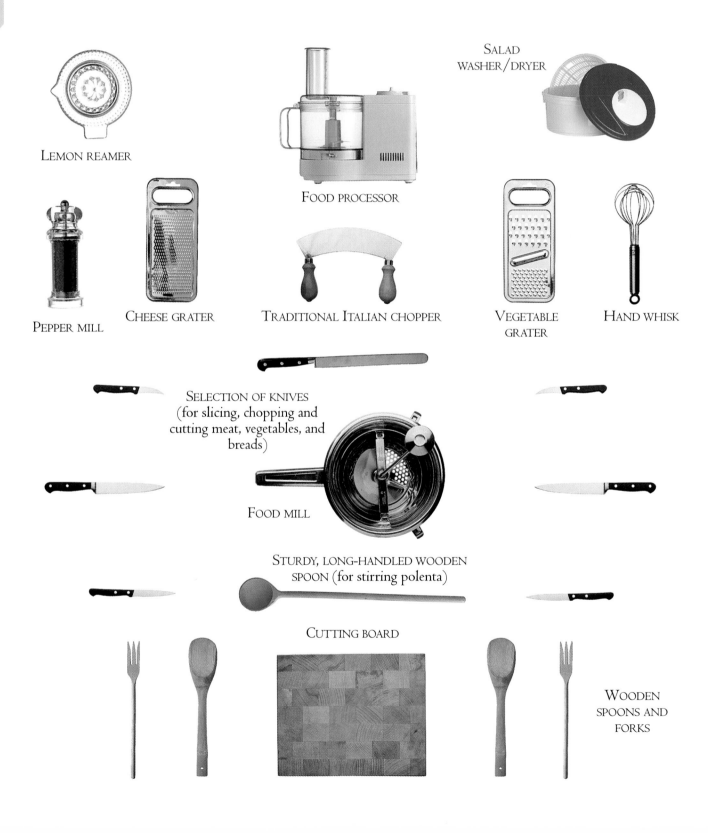

SALAD WASHER/DRYER

LEMON REAMER

FOOD PROCESSOR

PEPPER MILL

CHEESE GRATER

TRADITIONAL ITALIAN CHOPPER

VEGETABLE GRATER

HAND WHISK

SELECTION OF KNIVES (for slicing, chopping and cutting meat, vegetables, and breads)

FOOD MILL

STURDY, LONG-HANDLED WOODEN SPOON (for stirring polenta)

CUTTING BOARD

WOODEN SPOONS AND FORKS

NONSTICK SKILLET
(for crêpes)

OVENPROOF DISH

LIGHTWEIGHT ALUMINUM
SKILLET

ELECTRIC POLENTA
CAULDRON

SAUTÉ PANS

EARTHENWARE POT

LARGE POT
(with close-fitting lid)

LARGE POT
(for making polenta)

SELECTION OF SMALL POTS
AND SAUCEPANS
(with close-fitting lids)

GRILL PAN
(for grilling vegetables,
fish and meat indoors
with less fat)

SELECTION OF SKILLETS
(with close-fitting lids)

BASIC RECIPES

BRUSCHETTA ALLA ROMANA
Toasted bread with garlic, salt and oil

■ INGREDIENTS

- 4 large, thick slices bread
- 2 cloves garlic
- salt and freshly ground black pepper
- 4 tablespoons extra-virgin olive oil

Bruschetta is a classic Roman appetizer, although many regions of Italy have similar dishes. It can be difficult to recreate the authentic taste abroad because Roman bread is white, very compact, and unsalted. Be sure to choose bread that is not too fresh; yesterday's leftover loaf is best. You should toast the bread in the oven or under the broiler (or over a barbecue or open fire), rather than in the toaster. This will dry the bread out to just the right point.

Serves: 4; Preparation: 5 minutes; Cooking: 10 minutes; Level of difficulty: Simple

Toast the bread until golden brown on both sides. § Rub each slice with the garlic, sprinkle with salt and pepper, and drizzle with oil. § Serve hot.

VARIATION
– Toast the bread as above, omit the garlic, and serve with a selection of flavored oils. Make the oils by filling 5 small bottles with olive oil; add 1 teaspoon of crushed chilies to the first, a twig of fresh rosemary to the second, 2 bruised cloves of garlic to the third, 8 fresh mint leaves to the fourth, and 1 twig of fresh oregano to the fifth. (Experiment with other herbs and spices too). The oils should be prepared at least 1 day before serving so that they will have absorbed the flavor of the herb. Serve the toasted bread separately and let your guests help themselves to the oils as they please.

SALSA MAIONESE
Mayonnaise

■ INGREDIENTS

- 1 fresh egg yolk
- dash of salt
- ⅔ cup extra-virgin olive oil
- freshly ground black pepper
- 1 tablespoon lemon juice (or white vinegar)

Serves 4; Preparation: 15-20 minutes; Level of difficulty: Medium

BY HAND: use a fork or hand whisk to beat the egg yolk in a bowl with the salt. § Add the oil a drop at a time at first, then in a steady drizzle, stirring all the time in the same direction. § When the mayonnaise begins to thicken, add, very gradually, the lemon juice (or vinegar), pepper, and a few more drops of oil until it is the right density. § If the mayonnaise curdles, start over again with another egg yolk and use the curdled mayonnaise in place of the oil. IN THE BLENDER: use the same ingredients as above, except for the egg, which should be whole. § Place the egg, salt, pepper, 1-2 tablespoons of oil, and the lemon juice (or vinegar) in the blender and blend for a few seconds at maximum speed. § When the ingredients are well mixed, pour the remaining oil into the mixture very gradually. Blend until the right density is reached.

Right:
A selection of common Italian breads, all of which can be used to make crostini *or* bruschette. *Note the* bruschetta *in the foreground with garlic cloves on top.*

CROSTINI DI POLENTA
Preparing polenta for crostini

■ INGREDIENTS

- 4½ pints water
- 1 heaping tablespoon coarse sea salt
- 3½ cups coarse-grain cornmeal

This is a basic recipe for a firm polenta which will be ideal for making crostini *to spread with the various toppings suggested here and in the recipe section of this book. Making polenta is simple, although it is quite hard work. In Italy* crostini di polenta *are usually made with leftover polenta prepared the day before. For good* crostini, *you should prepare the polenta at least 12 hours before you intend to serve it; it needs time to settle and become firm before frying.*

Serves 8-12; Preparation 5 minutes + 12 hours resting; Cooking: 50-60 minutes; Level of difficulty: Simple

Bring the salted water to a boil in a heavy-bottomed pot large enough to hold 5 quarts. § Add the cornmeal gradually, stirring continuously and rapidly with a whisk so that no lumps form; polenta should always be perfectly smooth. § To cook, stir the polenta over high heat by moving a long, heavy wooden spoon in a circular motion. At a certain point the polenta will begin to withdraw from the sides of the pot on which a thin crust is forming. § The polenta should be stirred almost continuously for the 50-60 minutes it takes to cook. § Quantities and method are the same when using an electric polenta cauldron. Stir the cornmeal into the boiling water gradually, then turn on the mixer. Leave for 50-60 minutes. § Turn the polenta out on a board and set aside for about 12 hours to settle and become firm. § Cut into ½-inch thick slices and use as indicated in the recipes. § To make the *crostini* below, fry the polenta slices in hot oil for 6-8 minutes, or until golden brown on both sides.

TOPPINGS FOR POLENTA CROSTINI

— Prepare ½ quantity basic tomato sauce (see recipe p. 22). Add 1 tablespoon capers and spread over the fried *crostini.* Chop 4 ounces of mozzarella cheese in small dice and sprinkle on the *crostini.* Toast in a preheated oven at 400°F for 5-10 minutes. Serve hot.

— Prepare 1 quantity Tuscan-style or Country-style liver mixture (see p. 116). Spread the fried *crostini* with the liver mixture and serve hot or cold.

— Spread the fried *crostini* with 8 ounces soft cheese (gorgonzola, robiola, caprino, or other). Garnish with sprigs of parsley and serve.

— Thinly slice 8 ounces fontina cheese. Arrange on the slices of polenta, grind a little black pepper over the top. Toast in a preheated oven at 400°F for 5-10 minutes. Serve hot.

Right:
Crostini di polenta

BARCHETTE
Boat-shaped pastries

■ INGREDIENTS

• 2 cups all-purpose flour
• ⅔ cup butter
• 2-3 tablespoons cold water
• ½ teaspoon salt
• 3 cups dried beans

Barchette in Italian means "little boats" and refers to the shape of the molds traditionally used to prepare these little savory pastries. Freshly baked, they are delicious with all sorts of toppings and sauces. If you don't have boat-shaped molds on hand, use any small cake or other molds you have in the kitchen.

Serves: 4-6; Preparation: 15 minutes + 30 minutes resting; Cooking: 15 minutes; Level of difficulty: Simple

Sift the flour onto a counter, and work the flour and butter together with your fingertips until the mixture is the same texture as a coarse meal. § Make a well in the center and add the water and salt. Mix until you have a rather soft dough. § Form a ball, wrap in waxed paper, and set aside in a cool place for 30 minutes. § Flour the counter and, using a floured rolling pin, roll the dough out to about ⅛-inch thick. § Line the molds with the dough and prick the bottoms with a fork. Cover with pieces of waxed paper and fill with dried beans to stop the pastry rising too much during cooking. § Bake the *barchette* in a preheated oven at 350°F for 12-15 minutes. § Invert the molds, remove the waxed paper and beans, and set the *barchette* aside to cool. Use as indicated in the recipes, or invent new fillings.

SALSA BESCIAMELLA
Béchamel sauce

■ INGREDIENTS

• 2 cups milk
• ¼ cup butter
• ½ cup all-purpose flour
• salt

Béchamel sauce is used in many fillings for appetizers. It is quick and easy to prepare.

Serves 4; Preparation: 5 minutes; Cooking: 10 minutes; Level of difficulty: Simple

Heat the milk in a saucepan until it is almost boiling. § In a heavy-bottomed saucepan, melt the butter with the flour over low heat, stirring rapidly with a wooden spoon. Cook for about 1 minute. § Remove from the heat and add half the hot milk, stirring continuously. Return to low heat and stir until the sauce starts to thicken. § Add the rest of the milk gradually and continue stirring until it comes to a boil. § Season with salt to taste and continue stirring until the béchamel is the right thickness. § If any lumps form, beat the sauce rapidly with a fork or whisk until they dissolve.

Right:
Preparing barchette

Ragù di carne
Meat sauce

Simple, tasty, and versatile, this meat sauce can be used in a number of ways. Try it with the Malfatti di parmigiano e spinaci (see recipe p. 76), in the Parmigiana di zucchine (see recipe p. 78), spoon it over a platter of Polenta crostini (see recipe p. 18), or serve it over piping hot pasta or gnocchi.

Serves: 4-6; Preparation: 15 minutes; Cooking: at least 1½ hours; Level of difficulty: Simple

Sauté the onion, carrot, celery, and parsley in a skillet with the oil for 5 minutes. § Add the meat and mix well making sure that no lumps of meat form. Cook over medium heat for 5 minutes more. § Add the wine and when it has evaporated, stir in the tomatoes. § Cook for 10 minutes, then add the hot stock. § Season with salt and pepper. Cover and simmer over low heat for at least an hour. § Serve as indicated in the recipes.

■ INGREDIENTS

- 1 large onion, 1 large carrot, 1 stalk celery, finely chopped
- 1 tablespoon finely chopped parsley
- 4 tablespoons extra-virgin olive oil
- 1½ cups finely ground lean veal
- 1½ cups finely ground lean pork
- 1 glass dry red wine
- 1 cup meat stock made with boiling water and bouillon cube
- 1 14-ounce can peeled and chopped tomatoes
- salt and freshly ground black pepper

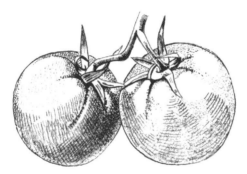

Pomarola
Basic tomato sauce

This recipe makes a fairly large quantity. It will keep well in the refrigerator for 4-5 days if you put it in an airtight container and pour a little olive oil over the top (a thin veil to cover the surface).

Serves: 6-8; Preparation: 15 minutes; Cooking: 50 minutes; Level of difficulty: Simple

Sauté the onion, carrot, celery, and garlic in a skillet with the oil for 5 minutes. § Add the tomatoes, parsley, basil, salt, pepper, and sugar. Partly cover and cook over medium-low heat for about 45 minutes, or until all the water has evaporated. § For a smoother sauce, press the mixture through a food mill. § Serve as indicated in the recipes.

■ INGREDIENTS

- 4 pounds fresh or canned tomatoes
- 1 large onion, 1 large carrot, 1 stalk celery, 1 clove garlic, coarsely chopped
- 1 tablespoon finely chopped parsley
- 8 fresh basil leaves, torn
- 4 tablespoons extra-virgin olive oil
- 1 teaspoon sugar
- salt and freshly ground black pepper

Right: *Preparing meat sauce*

Vegetable Appetizers

A salad or vegetable-based appetizer is a light and healthy way to begin a meal. A few of the recipes included in this chapter are fried or baked and thus heavier; in that case be sure to balance the meal by serving something light to follow.

Olive condite
Hot and spicy green olives

This tasty dish comes from Sicily. In some parts of the island the olives will sometimes appear on your table served in tiny, hollowed-out bread rolls. The crusty bread helps offset some of the fire in the dressing. Use only the highest quality green olives packed in brine.

Serves: 4; Preparation: 10 minutes + 2 hours to marinate; Level of difficulty: Simple

Rinse the olives in cold water and pat dry with paper towels. § Lightly crush the olives with a meat-pounding mallet. § Use the same instrument to bruise the cloves of garlic. Place the olives and garlic in a serving dish. § Remove the rosemary leaves from the twig and add to the olives, together with the mint, oregano, chilies, and oil. Mix well and cover. Set aside in a cool place (not the refrigerator) for at least 2 hours before serving. § Serve with lots of crusty bread.

VARIATION
– Add 2 tablespoons finely chopped scallions.

■ INGREDIENTS

- 2¼ cups pitted green olives
- 4 cloves garlic
- 1 twig fresh rosemary
- 1 tablespoon coarsely chopped fresh mint
- ½ teaspoon oregano
- ½ teaspoon crushed chilies
- 2 tablespoons extra-virgin olive oil

Wine: a dry white (Etna bianco)

Bruschetta con pomodori freschi
Bruschetta with fresh tomato topping

If you want to prepare this dish ahead of time, keep the bruschette *and tomato mixture separate until just before serving, otherwise the dish will become soggy and unappetizing.*

Serves: 4; Preparation: 10 minutes; Cooking: 10 minutes; Level of difficulty: Simple

Prepare the *bruschette*. § Dice the tomatoes into bite-size chunks. Place them in a bowl and mix with the oil, basil, oregano, salt and pepper. § Cover each bruschetta with a quarter of the tomato mixture. § Serve immediately.

VARIATIONS
– Add 1 cup diced mozzarella cheese to the tomato mixture.
– Add ⅓ teaspoon crushed chilies or 1 crumbled fresh chili to the tomato mixture.
– Add 1 tablespoon small salted capers to the tomato mixture.

■ INGREDIENTS

- 4 slices *bruschetta* (see recipe p. 16)
- 2 large ripe tomatoes
- 4 tablespoons extra-virgin olive oil
- 8 fresh basil leaves, torn
- 1 teaspoon oregano
- salt and freshly ground black pepper

Wine: a dry white (Orvieto Classico)

Right: *Olive condite*

■ INGREDIENTS

- 4 slices *bruschetta*
  (see recipe p. 16)
- 1-14 ounce can white
  beans
- salt and freshly ground
  black pepper
- 1 tablespoon extra-virgin
  olive oil

Wine: a dry, young red
(Vino Novello)

BRUSCHETTA CON FAGIOLI
Bruschetta with white beans

Serves: 4; Preparation: 10 minutes; Cooking: 10 minutes; Level of difficulty: Simple

Prepare the *bruschette*. § Heat the beans in a small saucepan. Taste for salt; season if necessary. § When hot, pour over the *bruschette*. § Sprinkle with pepper and drizzle with oil. § Serve hot.

VARIATIONS
– Add 6 fresh sage leaves to the beans when heating.
– For homemade baked beans; cook 2 large diced tomatoes in the saucepan before adding the beans. Serve hot.

CAROTE ALL'OLIO, AGLIO E LIMONE
Carrot salad with garlic, oil and lemon

*This light, refreshing, and vitamin-packed salad is a perfect
appetizer for hot summer evenings.*

Serves: 4; Preparation: 10 minutes + 30 minutes to marinate; Level of difficulty: Simple

Place the carrots, garlic, parsley, and mint in a small salad bowl. Add the lemon juice, oil, salt and pepper to taste. Mix well. § Set aside for at least 30 minutes before serving.

■ INGREDIENTS

- 4 large carrots, coarsely grated
- 1 clove garlic, finely chopped
- 2 tablespoons finely chopped parsley
- 1 tablespoon finely chopped mint leaves
- juice of 1 lemon
- 3 tablespoons extra-virgin olive oil
- salt and freshly ground black pepper

*Wine: a light, dry white
(Soave)*

PEPERONI ARROSTITI CON ACCIUGHE
Roasted bell peppers with anchovies

This dish is tastier if prepared the day before. Store in the refrigerator, but take out at least two hours before serving. If well covered with olive oil, roasted bell peppers with anchovies will keep for up to a week in the refrigerator.

Serves: 8; Preparation: 15 minutes + 2 hours to marinate; Cooking: 15-20 minutes; Level of difficulty: Simple

Cut the bell peppers in half lengthwise. Remove the seeds and pulpy core. Rinse under cold running water and pat dry with paper towels. Bake in a preheated oven at 400°F until the skins are wrinkled and slightly burned. Take the bell peppers out of the oven and leave to cool. Remove the charred skins with your fingers. § Cut the peeled bell peppers lengthwise into strips about 2 inches wide. Choose a serving dish that will hold 4-5 layers of bell peppers and line the bottom with one layer. § Crumble 4 of the anchovy fillets in a small mixing bowl and add the garlic, parsley, capers, oregano, and oil. § Place a layer of this mixture over the bell peppers. Cover with another layer of bell peppers and anchovy mixture. Repeat the procedure until all the ingredients have been used. § Garnish the top layer with the remaining anchovy fillets and the basil. Set the dish aside to marinate for at least 2 hours before serving.

■ INGREDIENTS

- 2 yellow, 2 green, and 2 red bell peppers, medium-size
- 8 anchovy fillets
- 4 cloves garlic, finely chopped
- 2 tablespoons finely chopped parsley
- 2 tablespoons capers
- ½ teaspoon oregano
- 4 tablespoons extra-virgin olive oil
- 8 fresh basil leaves, torn

*Wine: a dry red
(Chianti Classico)*

Right:
Peperoni arrostiti con acciughe

Zucchine grigliate con menta fresca e aglio
Grilled zucchini with fresh mint and garlic

■ INGREDIENTS

• 8 zucchini
• 12 tablespoons extra-virgin olive oil
• salt
• 2 tablespoons finely chopped parsley
• 1 tablespoon finely chopped fresh mint
• mixed red, black, green peppercorns
• 2 cloves garlic, finely chopped

*Wine: a dry white
(Trebbiano di Lugana)*

Serves 4; Preparation: 20 minutes + 2 hours to cool; Cooking: 10 minutes; Level of difficulty: Simple

Wash and dry the zucchini, trim the ends, and cut lengthwise into ¼-inch thick slices. § Heat the grill pan to very hot and cook the slices for 2-3 minutes on each side. Remove and set aside to cool. § Put the oil in a bowl with the salt, parsley, and mint, and beat with a fork or whisk until well mixed. § Arrange the cold zucchini slices in a small, fairly deep-sided serving dish. Sprinkle with the garlic and grind the mixed pepper over the top. § Pour the oil mixture over the zucchini (make sure that the zucchini are well-covered with oil) and refrigerate for at least 2 hours before serving.

VARIATIONS
– Sprinkle 6 crumbled anchovy fillets over the zucchini together with the garlic.
– For a spicy dish, add ½ teaspoon crushed chilies to the oil and mix with the parsley, mint, and salt.

Zucchine crude con maionese piccante
Marinated zucchini with spicy mayonnaise

■ INGREDIENTS

• 4 large zucchini
• 4 tablespoons white wine vinegar
• salt and freshly ground black pepper
• 1 quantity mayonnaise (see recipe p. 16)
• 2 teaspoons hot mustard
• 8 sprigs parsley

*Wine: a dry white
(Traminer aromatico)*

Serves 4; Preparation: 20 minutes + 2 hours to marinate; Level of difficulty: Simple

Wash and dry the zucchini, trim the ends, and slice thinly (skin and all). § Place in a bowl, add the vinegar, and sprinkle with salt. Mix well and leave to marinate for at least 2 hours. § Prepare the mayonnaise and stir in the mustard. § Drain the zucchini, squeeze them gently in your hands to remove as much vinegar as possible. § Mix the zucchini with the spicy mayonnaise and transfer to a serving dish. § Garnish with sprigs of parsley and serve.

*Right: Zucchine grigliate
con menta fresca e aglio*

INSALATA DI OVOLI
Caesar's mushroom salad

This eyecatching salad calls for very fresh Caesar's (also known as royal agaric) mushrooms. For a perfect salad, choose the ones with the caps still closed around the stems and serve them the same day they are purchased. They must be absolutely fresh.

Serves 4-6; Preparation: 10 minutes; Level of difficulty: Simple

Clean the mushrooms and rinse them carefully in cold water. Pat dry with paper towels. § Slice the mushrooms finely and arrange them on a serving dish. § Sprinkle with the walnuts and parmesan flakes. § Mix the oil, salt, pepper, and lemon juice in a bowl and pour over the mushrooms. § Serve immediately, or the flavor will begin to change.

VARIATIONS
– Add a finely chopped clove of garlic to the olive oil dressing.
– Replace the Caesar's mushrooms with the same quantity of closed white button mushrooms. In this case, serve on a bed of fresh, crisp arugula (rocket).

■ INGREDIENTS

• 14 ounces Caesar's (royal agaric) mushrooms
• 1 cup shelled and chopped walnuts
• 1 cup parmesan cheese, flaked
• 6 tablespoons extra-virgin olive oil
• salt and freshly ground white pepper
• juice of 1 lemon

Wine: a dry, sparkling white (Asti Spumante brut)

CROSTONI CON UOVA E FUNGHII
Crostoni with eggs and mushrooms

Serves 4; Preparation: 10 minutes; Cooking: 15 minutes; Level of difficulty: Simple

Clean the mushrooms, wash them carefully, and pat dry with paper towels. § Slice the mushrooms and sauté in a skillet with half the butter and the thyme for about 10 minutes. § Add the ham and season with salt just before removing from heat. Mix well. § Toast the bread in the oven or under the broiler and set aside in a warm place. § Melt the remaining butter in a saucepan over medium-low heat, break in the eggs, and let them set slightly before breaking them up with a fork. Continue cooking and stirring until the eggs are cooked but still soft. Season with salt. § Arrange the toasted bread on a serving dish and cover each slice with a quarter of the egg mixture, followed by a quarter of the mushroom mixture. § Sprinkle with the parsley and pepper and serve.

■ INGREDIENTS

• 4 ounces white mushrooms
• 3 tablespoons butter
• 1 teaspoon finely chopped fresh or ½ teaspoon dry thyme
• 3 ounces ham
• salt and freshly ground black pepper
• 4 large slices white or wholewheat bread
• 4 eggs
• 1 tablespoon finely chopped parsley

Wine: a dry red (Sangiovese di Romangna)

Right: *Insalata di ovoli*

FUNGHI INSAPORITI
Tasty braised mushrooms

- 1¼ pounds white mushrooms
- 4 cloves garlic, finely chopped
- 8 tablespoons extra-virgin olive oil
- 1 bay leaf
- 2 cloves
- 10 black peppercorns
- ⅓ cup dry white wine
- salt
- juice of 1 lemon

Wine: a dry white (Orvieto)

Serves 4; Preparation: 10 minutes; Cooking: 20 minutes; Level of difficulty: Simple

Clean the mushrooms. Wash and dry them carefully, then peel and slice. § Sauté the garlic in a skillet with the oil for 2-3 minutes, then add the mushrooms, bay leaf, cloves, and peppercorns. § Cook over high heat for a few minutes, then add the wine, lemon juice, and salt. § Cover the skillet and finish cooking over medium-low heat. § Transfer the mushrooms to a serving dish and serve either hot or cold with fresh crunchy bread or toast.

Teglia di verdure ripiene al forno
Platter of stuffed vegetables

■ INGREDIENTS

- 6 round zucchini
- 3 medium onions
- 3 medium tomatoes
- 1 red, 1 green, and 1 yellow bell pepper
- 3 eggs
- 2 cups bread crumbs
- 3 tablespoons finely chopped parsley
- 3 cloves garlic, finely chopped
- 8 tablespoons freshly grated parmesan cheese
- salt and freshly ground black pepper
- 6 tablespoons extra-virgin olive oil

Serves 6-8; Preparation: 15 minutes; Cooking: 40-50 minutes; Level of difficulty: Simple

Blanch the zucchini in salted water for 5 minutes, drain, and cool. Cut in half horizontally, scoop out the pulp, and set aside. § Peel the onions and blanch in salted water for 5 minutes, drain, and cool. § Cut the onions in half horizontally and hollow them out, leaving ½-inch thick sides. Chop the pulp and set aside. § Wash the tomatoes and cut them in half. Scoop out the pulp, and set aside. Be careful not to pierce the skin. § Cut the bell peppers in half and remove the seeds and core. § Beat the eggs in a bowl and add the bread crumbs, parsley, garlic, 6 tablespoons of parmesan, salt and bell pepper. § Stir in about half the tomato, zucchini, and onion pulp. Mix well until the mixture is smooth. § Fill the vegetables with the mixture and sprinkle with the remaining parmesan. § Pour the oil into a large ovenproof dish and arrange the vegetables in it. § Cook in a preheated oven at 400°F for 30-40 minutes. § Serve piping hot.

Wine: a dry white (Soave Classico)

Insalata di pomodori e basilico
Tomato and basil salad

■ INGREDIENTS

- 1 clove garlic
- 6 large tomatoes, firm and ripe
- salt and freshly ground black pepper
- 15 fresh basil leaves, torn
- dash of oregano
- 6 tablespoons extra-virgin olive oil

Tomato and basil salad is simple and typical of Italian summer cookery. It makes a tasty appetizer, a great side dish, or can be served between courses to revive the palate. Choose only the tastiest red tomatoes, and dress with the highest quality oil and the freshest of basil leaves.

Serves 4; Preparation: 15 minutes; Level of difficulty: Simple

Peel the garlic and rub the insides of a salad bowl with the clove stuck on a fork. § Wash, dry, and slice the tomatoes. Remove the seeds. § Sprinkle the slices with a little salt and place on a slightly inclined cutting board. Leave them for about 10 minutes so the water they produce can drain away. § Transfer to the salad bowl and sprinkle with the basil. § In a small bowl, beat the oregano, salt, pepper, and oil with a fork until well mixed. § Pour over the tomatoes and toss quickly. § Cover and set aside for about 15 minutes before serving.

Wine: a dry, slightly sparkling white (Verdicchio)

Right:
Teglia di verdure ripiene al forno

INSALATA AL GORGONZOLA
*Fennel, celery and carrots with apple
and gorgonzola sauce*

■ INGREDIENTS

- 2 fennel bulbs
- 2 carrots
- 1 celery plant
- 1 Granny Smith apple
- 1 clove garlic, finely chopped
- salt and freshly ground black pepper
- 3 tablespoons of extra-virgin olive oil
- 5 ounces mild gorgonzola
- 1 tablespoon finely chopped parsley

*Wine: a dry white
(Tocai di San Martino della
Battaglia)*

Serves 6; Preparation: 15 minutes; Level of difficulty: Simple

Discard the outer leaves of the fennel and halve the bulbs. Wash and cut into ⅛-inch thick slices. § Trim the carrots, scrape, and cut in julienne strips. § Trim the celery, removing any damaged or tough outer leaves, and cut the stalks in slices like the fennel. § Wash the apple and cut in thin wedges. § Put the garlic, apple, and vegetables in a salad bowl and season with salt, pepper, and 2 tablespoons of olive oil. § Dice the gorgonzola and put it in a heavy-bottomed saucepan with 1 tablespoon of oil. Melt slowly over low heat, stirring continuously. § When it is barely lukewarm and has become creamy, pour it over the vegetables. § Sprinkle with the parsley and serve.

COSTE DI SEDANO FARCITE
Celery stalks filled with gorgonzola and ricotta

■ INGREDIENTS

- 5 ounces gorgonzola
- 7 ounces ricotta
- 4-5 tablespoons milk
- 1 small onion, very finely chopped
- dash of paprika
- 1 tablespoon extra-virgin olive oil
- 1 tablespoon celery, finely chopped
- salt and freshly ground black pepper
- 12 celery stalks
- 8 sprigs parsley

*Wine: a young, dry white
(Vermentino Ligure)*

Serves 4-6; Preparation: 15 minutes + 1 hour in the refrigerator; Level of difficulty: Simple

Melt the gorgonzola in a heavy-bottomed saucepan over very low heat. § Remove from the heat when lukewarm and melted and add the ricotta and enough milk to obtain a creamy but dense mixture. § Add the onion, paprika, oil, finely chopped celery, salt and pepper. Mix well until smooth. § Cover and place in the refrigerator for about an hour. § Prepare the celery, removing the outer stalks and any stringy fibers. Rinse under cold running water, dry and slice into pieces about 2 inches long. § Fill the celery stalks with the mixture and arrange on a serving dish. Garnish with the parsley and serve.

VARIATIONS
– Replace the onion with 1 tablespoon finely chopped mint, 1 tablespoon finely chopped parsley, and 1 finely chopped garlic clove.
– Slice a crisp, tangy eating apple into wedges and arrange on the serving dish with the celery.

Left: Insalata al gorgonzola

Insalata invernale
Winter salad

This simple salad makes an excellent, light appetizer. For a richer dish, add a few sliced button mushrooms or diced mozzarella cheese. For best results, season with the mayonnaise just before serving.

Serves 4-6; Preparation: 30 minutes; Level of difficulty: Simple

Trim the artichokes and remove all leaves except the tender ones near the heart. Remove the tough outer leaves from the fennel bulb. § Wash and dry the artichoke and fennel hearts and cut in thin strips. § Peel the eggs and cut in thin slices. § Clean, wash, and slice the radishes. § Put all the vegetables in a bowl and season with the oil, salt, pepper, and vinegar. Toss well. § Prepare the mayonnaise. Using a hand whisk, mix the mayonnaise and cream. § Transfer the salad to a bowl, arrange the eggs on top, and dress with the mayonnaise. § Garnish with the parsley and serve immediately.

■ INGREDIENTS

- 3 globe artichokes
- 1 fennel bulb
- 3 hard-cooked eggs
- 10 radishes
- 2 tablespoons extra-virgin olive oil
- salt and freshly ground black pepper
- 1 tablespoon white wine vinegar
- 1 quantity mayonnaise (see recipe p. 16)
- 3 tablespoons light cream
- few sprigs parsley, for garnish

Wine: a dry white (Orvieto Classico)

Crostoni con asparagi
Crostoni with asparagus and orange sauce

Serves 6-8; Preparation: 30 minutes; Cooking: 30 minutes; Level of difficulty: Medium

Clean the asparagus, trim the stalks, and cook in a pot of salted, boiling water for 8-10 minutes. § Drain well and cut off all but the very tenderest part of the stalks and tips. § Squeeze the orange and set the juice aside. Cut half the rind into thin strips. § Blanch in a pot of boiling water for a few seconds. Drain and dry with paper towels. § Toast the bread and transfer to a serving dish. § Arrange the asparagus on the toast. § To prepare the sauce: place a large pan of water over medium heat. § Combine the egg yolks with a few pieces of butter, a dash of salt, and 1 tablespoon of water in a small pot. Beat well with a whisk. § Put the small pot in the larger one filled with water, keeping the heat low so the water doesn't boil. § As soon as the butter begins to melt, add the rest a little at a time, so that it is gradually absorbed, whisking all the time and taking care that the sauce never boils. § When the sauce is whipped and creamy, add another pinch of salt and, very gradually, the orange juice, stirring carefully all the time. § Remove from the heat and stir in the sliced orange rind. § Pour the orange sauce over the *crostoni* and serve immediately.

■ INGREDIENTS

- 3½ pounds asparagus
- 1 orange
- 12 slices plain or wholewheat bread
- 3 egg yolks
- ⅔ cup butter, cut in small pieces
- salt

Wine: a dry white (Albano di Romagna)

Right:
Insalata di cetrioli e cipolle

INGREDIENTS

- 5 medium sweet red onions
- salt and freshly ground black pepper
- 4 tablespoons extra-virgin olive oil
- 1 tablespoon white wine vinegar
- 2 medium cucumbers
- 1 tablespoon capers
- 6 leaves fresh basil, torn

Wine: a dry white (Cirò)

INSALATA DI CETRIOLI E CIPOLLA
Cucumber and onion salad

This refreshing summer salad comes from Calabria, in the south of Italy. It is really delicious when served with fresh ricotta or caprino cheese.

Serves 4-6; Preparation: 15 minutes + 30 minutes resting; Level of difficulty: Simple

Peel the onions and slice in thin wheels. § Put the onions in a salad bowl, sprinkle with the salt, pepper, vinegar, and oil. Toss well and set aside for 30 minutes. § Peel the cucumbers and slice very thinly. § Add the cucumbers and capers to the onions and toss well. § Garnish with the basil and serve.

Insalata di pere e peperoni
Pear and bell pepper salad

This salad can be made using bell peppers of one color, but it will be more attractive and appetizing if you use the three different colors. Always choose fresh, fleshy bell peppers and firm, ripe pears. The salad must be served as soon as it is made, otherwise the pears will turn black.

Serves 4-6; Preparation: 15 minutes; Level of difficulty: Simple

Clean the bell peppers by removing the top, seeds, and core. § Wash and cut in short, thin strips. § Peel and core the pears and cut into match-size sticks. § Combine the pear and bell pepper strips in a salad bowl, and add the garlic, salt, pepper, parsley, and oil. § Serve immediately.

■ INGREDIENTS

- 3 medium bell peppers (1 red, 1 yellow, 1 green)
- 2 firm ripe pears
- 1 clove garlic, finely chopped (optional)
- salt and freshly ground black pepper
- 1 tablespoon finely chopped parsley
- 4 tablespoons extra-virgin olive oil

Wine: a dry, sparkling white (Asti Spumante)

Erbazzone emiliano
Vegetable omelet Emilia-Romagna style

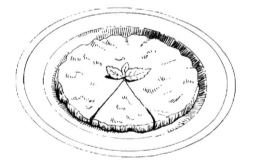

Serves 4-6; Preparation: 15 minutes; Cooking: 30 minutes; Level of difficulty: Simple

Clean and wash the greens. Cook them in a pot of salted, boiling water for 8-10 minutes. § Drain well, squeeze out excess water, and chop finely. § Sauté the garlic, parsley, and onion in the lard (or butter) over medium heat until the onion is transparent. § Add the greens, season with salt and pepper, and cook for 5 minutes more. § In a bowl, beat the eggs until foamy, mix in the vegetables, and then add the parmesan, flour, and bread crumbs. § Heat the oil in a large skillet and add the mixture, taking care to spread it evenly in the pan. § Cook until it begins to turn brown underneath, then carefully detach it from the sides of the skillet using a wooden spoon and turn it over (with the help of a lid or plate). Brown on the other side. § Slide onto a serving dish and serve hot.

■ INGREDIENTS

- 1¾ lb mixed fresh spinach and Swiss chard
- 4 cloves garlic, finely chopped
- 1¼ cups finely chopped parsley
- 1 small onion, finely chopped
- ⅓ cup lard or butter
- salt and freshly ground black pepper
- 4 eggs
- 1 cup freshly grated parmesan cheese
- 2 tablespoons all-purpose flour
- 2 tablespoons bread crumbs
- 4 tablespoons extra-virgin olive oil

Wine: a young, dry red (Gutturnio dei Colli Piacentini)

Right:
Erbazzone Emiliano

■ INGREDIENTS

- 7 ounces lollo rosso (or
  other leafy salad)
- 7 ounces arugula (rocket)
- salt and freshly ground
  black pepper
- 6 tablespoons canned
  peas, well-drained
- 8 ounces white mushrooms
- 1¼ cups emmental cheese,
  diced
- 8 tablespoons extra-virgin
  olive oil
- 1 tablespoon white wine
  vinegar
- 4 hard-cooked eggs, sliced
- 1 carrot, grated
- 8 radishes, finely sliced
- 1 tablespoon mustard
- 1 white truffle (optional)

Wine: a light, dry, sparkling
white (Prosecco)

■ INGREDIENTS

- 1 pound day-old bread
- 5 medium tomatoes
- 2 red onions
- 1 cucumber
- 12 leaves fresh basil, torn
- 6 tablespoons extra-virgin
  olive oil
- salt and freshly ground
  black pepper
- 1 tablespoon red wine
  vinegar

Wine: a dry red
(Chianti dei Colli Senesi)

Left: *Panzanella*

Insalata arcobaleno
Rainbow salad

*If you like truffles, slice a white one very thinly and add it to the mushrooms.
The salad will be even more fragrant and tasty.*

Serves 4-6; Preparation: 20 minutes; Level of difficulty: Simple

Wash and dry the salad greens and cut in strips. § Arrange in the bottom of a salad bowl and season with salt and pepper. § Sprinkle the peas over the top. § Clean, wash, peel, and thinly slice the mushrooms. Place them in a bowl with the cheese. § Prepare a dressing by beating the oil, mustard, salt, and vinegar together in a bowl. Pour half of it over the mushrooms and toss well. § Sprinkle the mushroom mixture over the salad and cover with the eggs, carrots, and radishes. § Just before serving, drizzle with the remaining dressing and toss again. § Serve immediately.

Panzanella
Tuscan bread salad

Panzanella is a typical Tuscan dish. The ingredients used vary according to which part of Tuscany it is made in. The addition of cucumber, for example, is shunned in the area around Siena, while it is always included in Florence. The salad can be enriched by adding diced carrots, fennel, celery, hard-cooked eggs, capers, or pecorino cheese.

Serves 4-6; Preparation: 15 minutes + 15 minutes resting; Level of difficulty: Simple

Soak the bread in a bowl of cold water for at least 10 minutes. § Use your hands to squeeze out as much water as possible. Crumble the almost dry bread into a large salad bowl. § Slice the tomatoes and remove the seeds. Clean the onions and slice in thin wheels. Peel the cucumber and slice thinly. § Add the tomatoes, cucumber, basil, and onions to the bread. Season with salt, pepper, and 4 tablespoons of the oil and mix carefully. § Set aside in a cool place or the refrigerator for 15 minutes. § Add the vinegar and remaining oil just before serving.

INSALATA DI FUNGHI PORCINI
Porcini mushroom salad

This mouthwatering salad is often served in Italy during the early summer months when porcini mushrooms are readily available. If you can't get porcini, you may want to experiment with other types of wild or cultivated mushrooms.

Serves 6; Preparation: 15 minutes; Level of difficulty: Simple

Clean the mushrooms, peel, rinse carefully under cold running water, and pat dry. § Without peeling, cut them in thin slices. § Wash the celery, remove any stringy fibers, and slice thinly. § Wash the lettuce hearts and slice thinly. § Place the lettuce in the bottom of a salad bowl and arrange the celery and mushrooms over the top. Cover with the parmesan. § In a small bowl, beat the oil, lemon juice, salt and pepper together with a fork. § Pour over the salad, toss carefully, and serve.

VARIATION
– Add ¾ cup of diced prosciutto and toss well.

■ INGREDIENTS

- 1 pound fresh porcini mushrooms
- 6 stalks celery
- 2 lettuce hearts
- 1 cup parmesan cheese, flaked
- 8 tablespoons extra-virgin olive oil
- juice of 1 lemon
- salt and freshly ground black pepper

Wine: a dry, young red (Vino Novello)

FUNGHI ALLE SPEZIE
Mushrooms with bay leaf, cinnamon and garlic

Serves 4; Preparation: 25 minutes; Cooking: 20 minutes; Level of difficulty: Simple

Clean the mushrooms, peel, rinse under cold running water, and pat dry. § Put the bay leaf, cinnamon, and half the lemon juice in a pot full of water and bring to a boil. § Add the mushrooms and boil for 2-3 minutes. Drain well and cut the mushrooms in half. § Transfer to a skillet with the oil, the remaining lemon juice, salt, and peppercorns, and cook for 15 minutes. § Remove from the heat, drain, and set aside to cool. § Sprinkle with the parsley and garlic, and serve.

■ INGREDIENTS

- 1¼ pounds button mushrooms
- 1 bay leaf
- 1 cinnamon stick
- juice of 1 lemon
- 6 tablespoons extra-virgin olive oil
- salt
- 10 black peppercorns, bruised
- ¾ cup finely chopped parsley
- 1 clove garlic, finely chopped

Wine: a dry, sparkling red (Lambrusco di Sorbara)

Right:
Insalata di funghi porcini

INGREDIENTS

- 12 slices mozzarella cheese
- 12 slices firm red tomato
- 1½ cups mixed vegetables (onion, bell pepper, celery, zucchini, carrots, finely chopped)
- 1 tablespoon capers
- 1 tablespoon extra-virgin olive oil
- salt and freshly ground black pepper
- 6 leaves fresh basil, torn

Mozzarella e pomodoro con verdure fresche
Mozzarella and tomato slices with fresh vegetables

These eyecatching mozzarella and vegetable slices make a light and tasty start to any meal. If you like garlic, add a clove (very finely chopped) to the vegetable mixture.

Serves 4-6; Preparation: 10 minutes; Level of difficulty: Simple

Arrange the slices of mozzarella on a serving dish and cover each one with a slice of tomato. § Combine the chopped vegetables in a bowl with the capers, salt, pepper, and oil. § Spread the vegetable mixture over the tomato. § Garnish with the basil and serve.

Olive alla marchigiana
Stuffed olives

This dish requires time and patience but these delicious little olives are so good that you will be tempted to make them again and again. The recipe comes from the Marches area in central Italy.

Serves 4-6; Preparation: 30 minutes; Cooking: 40 minutes; Level of difficulty: Medium

Sauté the beef and pork in a skillet with the olive oil for 5 minutes. Add the tomato paste and continue cooking for 15 minutes. § Add the chicken livers and cook for 5 minutes more. § Remove from heat, chop the meat very finely, and return to the skillet. § Soak the bread roll in cold water, squeeze out excess moisture, and crumble. § Add the bread, one of the eggs, the parmesan, salt, pepper, nutmeg, and cinnamon to the meat mixture. § Mix well with a fork and then stuff the pitted olives. § Arrange three bowls, the first with the flour, the second with 2 beaten eggs, and the third with the bread crumbs. § Dredge the olives in the flour, dip them in the egg and then in the bread crumbs. Remove excess crumbs by rolling them in your hands. § Deep-fry in a skillet with the frying oil. When a crisp, golden crust forms around each olive, remove from the pan with a slotted spoon. Place them on paper towels to drain excess oil. § Transfer to a serving dish, garnish with slices of lemon and parsley, and serve hot.

■ INGREDIENTS

- 1¼ cups pork, coarsely chopped
- 1¼ cups beef, coarsely chopped
- 4 tablespoons extra-virgin olive oil
- 2 tablespoons tomato paste
- ⅔ cup chicken livers, coarsely chopped
- 1 day-old bread roll
- 3 eggs
- 5 tablespoons freshly grated parmesan cheese
- salt and freshly ground black pepper
- dash of nutmeg
- dash of cinnamon
- 60 giant green olives, pitted
- 1¼ cups all-purpose flour
- 2½ cups bread crumbs
- 2 cups oil, for frying
- 1 lemon, sliced
- 8 sprigs parsley

Wine: a dry, young red (Rosso Conero)

Pomodorini cremosi
Cherry tomatoes filled with caprino cheese

Serves 4-6; Preparation: 30 minutes; Level of difficulty: Simple

Wash the tomatoes and dry well. § Turn them upside down and slice off a "lid." Set aside. § Using a small teaspoon, carefully remove the pulp. § Leave the tomatoes hole-side-down to drain for 10 minutes. § In a bowl, mix the oil, tomato pulp, olives, garlic, basil, salt, pepper, and cheese to a smooth cream. § Stuff the tomatoes with the filling. Place a "lid" on top of each and set aside in the refrigerator for 20 minutes before serving.

■ INGREDIENTS

- 12 cherry tomatoes
- ½ tablespoon extra-virgin olive oil
- 10 green olives, 1 clove garlic, finely chopped
- 6 fresh basil leaves, torn
- salt and freshly ground black pepper
- 8 ounces caprino cheese

Wine: a dry white (Verduzzo)

VARIATION
– For a lighter dish, use 8 ounces ricotta instead of caprino cheese.

Right: *Olive alla marchigiana*

POLENTA FRITTA SPLENDIDA
Fried polenta with mushroom, peas and cheese

Serves 4-6; Preparation: 15 minutes; Cooking: 30 minutes; Level of difficulty: Simple

Heat the oil in a skillet and add the mushrooms and peas. Mix well and cook over medium heat for 10 minutes. § Add the capers, salt and pepper. Cook for 5-10 minutes more, or until the vegetables are soft, stirring occasionally. § Lightly flour the polenta slices, dip them into the egg, and then into a bowl containing the bread crumbs. § Heat the frying oil in a deep-sided skillet until very hot and fry the slices of polenta until golden brown. § Drain on paper towels and arrange in a buttered baking dish. § Cover each slice with a spoonful of peas and mushrooms, and a slice of mozzarella. § Bake in a preheated oven at 400°F for about 10 minutes, or until the mozzarella is melted and golden. § Remove from the oven, sprinkle with the basil, and serve immediately.

■ INGREDIENTS

- 2 tablespoons extra-virgin olive oil
- 7 ounces white mushrooms, sliced
- 8 ounces fresh or frozen peas
- 1 tablespoon capers
- salt and freshly ground black pepper
- 4 tablespoons all-purpose flour
- 6 large slices cold polenta (see recipe p. 18)
- 1 egg, beaten
- 1 cup bread crumbs
- 2 cups oil, for frying
- 3½ ounces mozzarella cheese
- 4 tablespoons finely chopped basil

Wine: a dry red (Chianti Classico)

POLENTA FRITTA CON SALSA DI FUNGHI PORCINI
Fried polenta pieces with porcini mushroom sauce

Both recipes on this page will give you the chance to use up leftover polenta. If you can't get fresh porcini for this mushroom sauce, combine ¼ cup of soaked, dried porcini mushrooms with fresh white mushrooms. Even a small amount of porcini will flavor the other mushrooms.

Serves 6; Preparation: 30 minutes; Cooking: 40 minutes; Level of difficulty: Medium

Clean the mushrooms, rinse carefully under cold running water, and pat dry with paper towels. § Detach the stalks from the heads. § Sauté the garlic with the olive oil in a skillet over medium heat until golden brown. § Coarsely chop the mushrooms. § Add the stalks to the skillet first (they need longer to cook than the caps), and after about 5 minutes, add the caps. Add the calamint (or thyme) and season with salt and pepper. § Stir carefully for 4-5 minutes more. The time the porcini take to cook will depend on how fresh they are. Don't let them become mushy. § Heat the frying oil in a deep-sided skillet until very hot and fry the polenta slices until golden brown. § Spoon the mushroom sauce onto the polenta slices and serve hot.

■ INGREDIENTS

- 2 pounds fresh porcini mushrooms
- 2 cloves garlic, finely chopped
- 6 tablespoons extra-virgin olive oil
- 2 tablespoons finely chopped calamint or thyme
- salt and freshly ground black pepper
- 2 cups oil, for frying
- 6 large slices cold polenta (see recipe p. 18)

Wine: a dry red (Nobile di Montepulciano)

Right: *Polenta fritta con salsa di funghi porcini*

CROSTINI SICILIANI
Sicilian-style crostini

Serves 4; Preparation: 10 minutes; Cooking: 10 minutes; Level of difficulty: Simple

Cut the slices of bread in half and remove the crusts. § Heat the oil in a skillet and fry the bread until golden brown on both sides. § Drain on paper towels. § Bring the vinegar, sugar, and 2 tablespoons of water to a boil, then add the capers, pine nuts, raisins, candied lemon peel, and tomatoes. § Cook for 5 minutes, stirring with care. § Spread the fried *crostini* with this mixture and serve hot.

ARANCINI DI RISO
Rice croquettes

Serves 4-6; Preparation: 20 minutes; Cooking: 55 minutes; Level of difficulty: Medium

Cook the rice as you would a risotto, gradually stirring in the boiling stock as needed. When the rice is cooked, the liquid should all have been absorbed. § Sauté the onion in a skillet over medium heat with the oil until golden. § Wash the chicken livers, chop coarsely, and add to the skillet. Add the veal, peas, and wine. § When the liquid has evaporated, add the tomato pulp and season with salt and pepper. § Continue cooking, stirring often until the sauce is thick. § Combine the rice, parmesan, and butter in a bowl. § Mix well and mold into balls. Hollow out the center of each ball and fill with meat sauce and a piece of hard-cooked egg. § Close the rice around the filling. § Beat the raw eggs with a fork in a shallow dish. Dip the balls into the egg and then roll in bread crumbs. § Heat the oil in a deep-sided skillet and fry the balls until golden brown. § Drain on paper towels and serve piping hot.

■ INGREDIENTS

- 2 cups rice
- 1-2 cups meat stock
- 1 small onion, chopped
- 2 tablespoons extra-virgin olive oil
- ¾ cup chicken livers
- ½ cup ground veal
- 1½ cups peas
- 2 tablespoons white wine
- 2 tablespoons tomato pulp
- salt and freshly ground black pepper
- 2 tablespoons freshly grated parmesan cheese
- 2 tablespoons butter
- 2 hard-cooked eggs
- 2 eggs
- 1½ cups bread crumbs
- 2 cups oil, for frying

Wine: a dry red (Corvo Rosso)

CARCIOFI CON LA MOZZARELLA
Artichokes with mozzarella

Serves 4-6; Preparation: 20 minutes; Cooking: 40 minutes; Level of difficulty: Medium

Clean the artichokes by removing the stalks and tough outer leaves. Trim off the tops and place the hearts in a bowl of cold water with the lemon juice. § Mix the mozzarella with the parmesan, bread crumbs, and egg. Season with salt, pepper, and a tablespoon of oil. § Drain the artichokes, press out the water, dry, open and use a sharp knife to remove the centers. § Put some of the mozzarella mixture in each artichoke and set them upright, one next to the other, in an oiled braiser. § Pour the remaining oil over the top, add 2 glasses of water, cover and bring to a boil. § Transfer the braiser to a preheated oven at 350°F and cook the artichokes for about 40 minutes, basting them frequently with the liquid that settles in the bottom of the braiser. § Serve hot.

■ INGREDIENTS

- 8 globe artichokes
- juice of 1 lemon
- 1 cup mozzarella cheese, finely chopped
- 2 tablespoons freshly grated parmesan cheese
- 4 heaping tablespoons bread crumbs
- 1 egg
- salt and freshly ground black pepper
- ½ cup extra-virgin olive oil

Wine: a dry white (Corvo)

Right: *Arancini di riso*

Teste di funghi ripiene
Filled mushroom caps

Serves 4-6; Preparation: 30 minutes; Cooking: 30 minutes; Level of difficulty: Medium

Clean the mushrooms and carefully wash them under cold running water. Pat dry with paper towels and separate the stems from the caps. § Chop the stems, garlic, crumbled bread, salt and pepper together. § Transfer to a bowl and mix until the mixture has the consistency of a thick cream (add milk if it is too dry). § Stir in the eggs, parmesan, oregano, calamint (or thyme), and 1 tablespoon of oil. § Mix thoroughly and taste for salt. Fill the hollow of each mushroom cap with the mixture, and smooth the surface with a moistened knife blade. § Arrange the mushrooms in a lightly oiled ovenproof dish. § Drizzle with oil and bake in a preheated oven at 350°F for about 30 minutes. § Serve hot straight from the baking dish.

■ INGREDIENTS

- 12 Caesar's (royal agaric) mushrooms
- 1 clove garlic
- 2 slices bread, soaked in warm milk and crumbled
- salt and freshly ground black pepper
- 1 egg and 1 yolk
- 1 cup freshly grated parmesan cheese
- dash of oregano
- 3 sprigs calamint (or thyme)
- 4 tablespoons extra-virgin olive oil

Wine: a dry white (Albenga)

Strisce colorate
Mixed baked vegetables

This dish can be really eyecatching. Be sure to arrange the vegetables in strips—a strip of onions, followed by one of green bell peppers, then zucchini, tomatoes, eggplant, and lastly the yellow peppers. Not all the vegetable varieties are essential, but keep the idea of color in mind when choosing them and try to have at least two or three different colors.

Serves 4-6; Preparation: 30 minutes; Cooking: 1 hour; Level of difficulty: Medium

Wash the bell peppers, remove the seeds and cores, and cut into narrow strips, keeping the colors separate. § Clean the onions and cut into thin rings. § Cut the eggplant and the zucchini into julienne strips. § Cut the tomatoes in half, remove the seeds, and squeeze out excess water. Cut into small wedges. § Arrange the vegetables in strips (not layers), alternating the colors, in an ovenproof dish. § Season with salt and pepper, and drizzle with the oil. § Cover with aluminum foil and seal well around the edges of the dish. § Bake in a preheated oven at 325°F for about an hour. § Check the vegetables after 30 minutes and increase the heat if there is too much liquid or add a drop if they are too dry. When cooked, all the liquid should have been absorbed but the vegetables should not be dried out. § Serve hot or cold.

■ INGREDIENTS

- 1 yellow and 1 green bell pepper
- 2 onions
- 1 eggplant
- 2 zucchini
- 6 plum tomatoes
- salt and freshly ground black pepper
- 3 tablespoons extra-virgin olive oil

Wine: a light, dry white (Soave Classico)

Right:
Strisce colorati

Sformato di fagiolini
Green bean mold

INGREDIENTS

- 14 ounces fresh green beans
- 2 tablespoons extra-virgin olive oil
- ¼ cup butter
- ½ onion, finely chopped
- 1 stalk celery, finely chopped
- 1 tablespoon finely chopped parsley
- ½ bouillon cube
- ½ cup boiling water
- 4 tablespoons freshly grated parmesan cheese
- salt and freshly ground black pepper
- ½ quantity béchamel sauce (see recipe p. 20)
- 2 eggs, beaten
- 2 tablespoons bread crumbs

Serves 4-6; Preparation: 20 minutes; Cooking: 1¼ hours; Level of difficulty: Medium

Clean and wash the beans and cook for 10 minutes in lightly salted, boiling water. Drain and pass under cold running water. § Drain again and transfer to a dry kitchen towel. § Put the oil and half the butter in a skillet. Add the onion, celery, and parsley, and when the onion begins to turn golden, add the beans. § Sauté so the beans can absorb the seasoning. § Dissolve the bouillon cube in the water and add. § Cover the pan and simmer for about 20 minutes. § Add the parmesan and pepper to the béchamel sauce. § Drain the beans and transfer to a bowl. Add half the béchamel sauce and the eggs. Mix well. § Butter a mold and sprinkle with the bread crumbs. Fill with the beans and cover with the remaining béchamel sauce. § Place a large container of cold water in a preheated oven at 350°F. Place the mold pan in the water-filled container and cook *bain-marie* for 40 minutes. § Invert the mold onto a serving dish, slice and serve.

> VARIATIONS
> – Serve with 1 quantity of Basic tomato sauce (see recipe p. 22).
> – Add ¾ cup diced ham to the skillet with the beans.

Wine: a dry white (Bianco di Custoza)

Beignets di spinaci
Spinach fritters

INGREDIENTS

- ½ quantity béchamel sauce (see recipe p. 20)
- 1 pound frozen spinach
- 2 tablespoons butter
- 2 egg yolks + 1 whole egg
- dash of nutmeg
- salt and freshly ground pepper
- 2 cups oil, for frying

Serves 4-6; Preparation: 15 minutes; Cooking: 30 minutes; Level of difficulty: Simple

Prepare the béchamel sauce. § Put the spinach in a pot to defrost over medium-low heat. § When the liquid has evaporated, squeeze dry and chop coarsely. § Return to the pot, add the butter and sauté for 5 minutes. § Remove from the heat and transfer to a bowl. § Add the béchamel sauce and mix well. Add the eggs, one at a time, and then the nutmeg, salt and pepper. Mix again until smooth. § Heat the frying oil in a deep-sided skillet until hot. § Add a few spoonfuls of the spinach mixture to the oil. Keep them well-spaced. § Turn the fritters as they cook so they turn golden on all sides. § Remove with a slotted spoon and place on paper towels to drain. § Repeat until all the fritters are cooked. § Sprinkle with salt and serve hot.

Wine: a dry red (Chianti Montalbano)

Right:
Sformato di fagiolini

■ INGREDIENTS

• 8 barchette (see recipe p. 20)
• 1 quantity mayonnaise
  (see recipe p. 16)
• 2 hard-cooked eggs
• 1 tablespoon finely
  chopped parsley
• 1 tablespoon finely
  chopped marjoram
• 1 small white truffle

Wine: a dry white (Tocai di Lison)

BARCHETTE CON MAIONESE AGLI AROMI
Barchette with herb mayonnaise and truffles

Serves 4; Preparation: 15 minutes + time to make mayonnnaise and barchette; Level of difficulty: Simple
Prepare the *barchette* and set aside. § Prepare the mayonnaise. § Chop the eggs. § Transfer to a bowl and mix with the parsley, marjoram, and mayonnaise. § Fill the *barchette* with the sauce, arrange on a serving dish, and sprinkle with slivers of truffle. § Serve soon after filling so that the *barchette* are still crisp and fresh.

■ INGREDIENTS

- 4 large round tomatoes, ripe but firm
- salt and freshly ground black pepper
- 4 tablespoons finely chopped parsley
- 2 cloves garlic, finely chopped
- 1 cup bread crumbs
- 1 tablespoon capers
- dash of oregano
- 4 tablespoons extra-virgin olive oil

Wine: a dry white (Greco di Tufo)

Pomodori alla vesuviana
Baked Neapolitan-style tomatoes

Serves 4; Preparation: 20 minutes; Cooking: 30 minutes; Level of difficulty: Simple

Wash and dry the tomatoes and cut them in half horizontally. § Scoop out the seeds and part of the pulp and sprinkle the insides with a little salt and pepper. Turn them upside down and leave for 15 minutes to eliminate excess water. Pat dry with paper towels. § Combine the parsley, garlic, almost all the bread crumbs, capers, salt, pepper, and oregano in a bowl and mix well. § Fill the tomatoes with the mixture and arrange them in a well-oiled baking dish (use half the oil). § Drizzle with the remaining oil and bake in a preheated oven at 350°F for about 30 minutes. § Serve either hot or cold.

■ INGREDIENTS

- 1 Italian pork sausage
- 2 tablespoons butter
- 1 cup ground veal
- 4 large onions
- 2 eggs
- salt and freshly ground black pepper
- dash of nutmeg
- 6 tablespoons freshly grated parmesan cheese
- 1 tablespoon finely chopped parsley
- 1 macaroon, crumbled
- 1 tablespoon grappa
- 2 tablespoons bread crumbs

Wine: a dry red (Dolcetto d'Alba)

Left: *Cipolle ripiene dolce delicate*

Cipolle ripiene dolci delicate
Stuffed onions

Serves 4; Preparation: 15 minutes; Cooking: 1 hour; Level of difficulty: Simple

Peel and crumble the sausage and sauté in a skillet with half the butter. § Add the veal, stir well, and let brown slightly. Remove from the heat. § Peel the onions and cook for 10 minutes in a small pan of salted, boiling water. Drain well and pat dry with paper towels. § Cut the onions in half horizontally and carefully scoop out the center with a spoon. Chop the pulp finely and add to the meat and sausage mixture. § Stir in 1 egg, salt, pepper, nutmeg, 5 tablespoons of the parmesan, parsley, and the macaroon, and mix well. § Fill the onions with the mixture and arrange in a buttered baking dish. § Sprinkle with the grappa. § Beat the remaining egg to a foam and brush over the onions. Dust with the bread crumbs mixed with the remaining parmesan. Dab each onion with the remaining butter. § Bake in a preheated oven at 350°F for 45 minutes, or until a golden crust has formed on the surface. § Serve hot.

Egg and Cheese Appetizers

An almost endless variety of appetizers can be made using eggs and cheese. The following recipes are a selection of some personal favorites.

UOVA SODE CON SALSA DI PEPERONI
Hard-cooked eggs with bell pepper sauce

Serves 4-6; Preparation: 40 minutes; Cooking: 25-30 minutes; Level of difficulty: Simple

Combine the bell peppers, onion, garlic, parsley, and basil in a skillet with a dash of salt and the oil and sauté over medium heat. § To peel the tomatoes, bring a large pot of water to a boil. Plunge the tomatoes into the boiling water for 30 seconds and then transfer to cold water. The skins will slip off easily in your hands. § Cut the tomatoes in small dice and add to the saucepan. Cook over medium-low heat until the sauce is thick and smooth. § Add the vinegar and sugar, and mix well. Season with salt and pepper. § Remove from heat and set aside to cool. § Peel the hard-cooked eggs and cut in half lengthwise. § Remove the yolks, mash, and add to the tomato and bell pepper sauce. Mix well. § Fill the eggs with the mixture and arrange them on a serving dish. Pour any extra sauce over the top (or serve on slices of toasted bread or *bruschetta* with the eggs). § Place the eggs in the refrigerator for at least 30 minutes before serving.

■ INGREDIENTS

- 1 yellow and 1 red bell pepper, finely chopped
- 2 white onions, finely chopped
- 2 cloves garlic, finely chopped
- 1 tablespoon finely chopped parsley
- 1 tablespoon finely chopped fresh basil
- salt and freshly ground black pepper
- 2 tablespoons extra-virgin olive oil
- 6 fresh tomatoes
- 1 tablespoon vinegar
- ½ tablespoon sugar
- 6 hard-cooked eggs

Wine: a dry white
(Vernaccia di San Gimignano)

CROSTINI AI QUATTRO FORMAGGI
Crostini with four cheeses

The four cheeses given here are suggestions since all cheeses are delicious when toasted on bread. Replace them with your particular favorites or with what you have in the refrigerator. Cheese crostini also make a nourishing after-school or late night snack.

Serves 4; Preparation: 10 minutes; Cooking: 15 minutes; Level of difficulty: Simple

Combine the cheeses in a bowl with the oil. Season with salt, oregano, and marjoram. § Mash the cheeses with a fork and mix well until you have a fairly smooth cream. If the mixture is too thick to spread, add more oil. § Spread on the bread and cut each slice in half to form a triangle. Grind a little black pepper over the top. Arrange the *crostini* on a baking sheet. § Bake in a preheated oven at 400°F for 10-15 minutes, or until the cheese is golden brown. § Serve hot.

■ INGREDIENTS

- 4 ounces soft caprino cheese
- 1 cup freshly grated parmesan cheese
- 1 cup gorgonzola cheese, diced
- 1 cup fontina cheese, grated
- 2 tablespoons extra-virgin olive oil
- salt and freshly ground black pepper
- dash of oregano and marjoram
- 8 slices plain or wholewheat bread

Wine: a dry red (Lambrusco)

Right:
Uova sode con salsa di peperoni

INGREDIENTS

- ¼ cup butter
- 6 ounces ricotta cheese
- 6 ounces mascarpone cheese
- 6 ounces gorgonzola cheese
- 1 clove garlic, finely chopped
- 1 tablespoon cumin seeds
- 1 tablespoon finely chopped parsley
- 2 tablespoons brandy
- salt and freshly ground black pepper

FORMAGGI MISTI AL CUMINO
Mixed cheeses with cumin seeds

Serves 4; Preparation: 20 minutes + 4 hours in the refrigerator; Level of difficulty: Simple

Soften the butter over very low heat. § Combine the butter, ricotta, gorgonzola, mascarpone, garlic, cumin, parsley, and brandy in a bowl and mix well with a fork. Season with salt and pepper and continue mixing until smooth and creamy. § Place the mixture on a sheet of waxed paper and shape it into a log. § Wrap tightly in the paper and place in the refrigerator for at least 4 hours. § Unwrap and transfer to a serving dish. § Serve with fresh crunchy bread or toast.

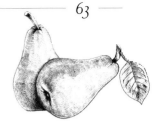

PERE CON GORGONZOLA DOLCE
Pears with gorgonzola cheese

■ INGREDIENTS

• 4 large eating pears
• juice of 2 lemons
• 5 ounces gorgonzola cheese
• 2 tablespoons fresh cream
• 4 tablespoons extra-virgin olive oil
• 1 tablespoon finely chopped mint, plus sprigs for garnishing
• salt and freshly ground white pepper

Wine: a dry white (Pinot Grigio)

Serves 4-6; Preparation: 25 minutes + 1 hour in the refrigerator; Level of difficulty: Simple

Wash the pears thoroughly, dry well, and remove the cores with a corer. § Brush the cavities with the juice of 1 lemon. § Combine the gorgonzola and cream in a bowl and mix until they form a smooth, thick cream. § Stuff the pears with the mixture, pressing it down so that the cavities are completely filled. § Place in the cold part of the refrigerator for at least an hour. § Combine the oil, remaining lemon juice, chopped mint, salt and pepper in a bowl and whisk until well mixed. § Use a sharp knife to cut the pears in thin round slices. § Arrange the rounds on individual serving dishes and spoon the sauce over the top. § Garnish with sprigs of mint and serve.

MOUSSE DI FORMAGGIO E NOCI
Cheese and walnut mousse

■ INGREDIENTS

• 3 large eating pears
• 7 ounces ricotta cheese
• 8 ounces mascarpone cheese
• 8 ounces gorgonzola cheese
• 2 cups walnuts, finely chopped
• freshly ground black pepper
• 2 tablespoons grappa
• 1 tablespoon butter
• 2 tablespoons finely chopped chives

Wine: a dry white (Soave)

Serves 6; Preparation: 15 minutes + 1 hour in the refrigerator; Level of difficulty: Simple

Wash the pears, peel, core, and chop the pulp finely. § Combine the cheeses in a bowl, mix, then add the walnuts, pepper, and grappa. § Stir the pear pulp into the cheese mixture. § Butter six small molds and fill with the mixture. Place in the refrigerator for at least an hour. § Just before serving, invert the molds onto serving plates and garnish with the chives.

INSALATA DI ZUCCHINE TENERE
Baby zucchini with pecorino cheese

■ INGREDIENTS

• 14 ounces baby zucchini
• 1¼ cups pecorino romano cheese, flaked
• 4 tablespoons extra-virgin olive oil
• salt and freshly ground black pepper

Wine: a dry white (Lugana)

Serves 4; Preparation: 30 minutes; Level of difficulty: Simple

Wash the zucchini, trim the ends, and slice them very thinly. § Transfer to a serving dish and sprinkle with the pecorino. § Pour the oil over the top and sprinkle with salt and pepper. § Toss well and serve.

> VARIATIONS
> – Replace the pecorino cheese with the same quantity of parmesan.
> – Add the juice of 1 lemon together with the oil.

Left: *Pere con gorgonzola dolce*

PEPERONI RIPIENI DI PARMIGIANO E RICOTTA
Bell peppers filled with parmesan and ricotta

Be sure to choose rounded bell peppers that will sit upright in the baking dish during cooking.

Serves 4; Preparation: 15 minutes; Cooking: 35 minutes; Level of difficulty: Simple

Cut the tops off the bell peppers and discard the seeds and cores. § Wash them carefully under cold running water and pat dry with paper towels. § Combine the bread crumbs, parsley, mint, garlic, and parmesan in a food processor and blend until smooth. § Transfer the mixture to a large bowl and stir in the eggs and ricotta. Season with salt, pepper, and oil, and mix until smooth. § Fill the peppers with the mixture and arrange them in an ovenproof dish. § Cover with knobs of butter and cook in a preheated oven at 400°F for about 35 minutes, or until the bell peppers are cooked. § Serve hot or cold.

VARIATION
– For a more substantial dish, add 1 cup finely chopped ham to the bread and parmesan mixture.

■ INGREDIENTS

- 4 yellow bell peppers
- 1 cup bread crumbs
- 1 tablespoon finely chopped parsley
- 4 finely chopped mint leaves
- 1 clove garlic, finely chopped
- 1 cup freshly grated parmesan cheese
- 2 eggs, beaten
- 7 ounces ricotta cheese
- salt and freshly ground black pepper
- 2 tablespoons extra-virgin olive oil
- 3 tablespoons butter

Wine: a dry red (Carmignano)

RICCI DI GORGONZOLA E SEDANO
Gorgonzola and celery served "porcupine-style"

Serves 4-6; Preparation: 20 minutes + 1 hour in the refrigerator; Level of difficulty: Simple

Melt the butter in a saucepan over low heat. § Combine the butter and gorgonzola in a bowl and mix well. § Gradually add the oil, lemon juice, and pepper, and stir carefully with a wooden spoon until the mixture becomes a thick cream. § Transfer the cheese mixture to a small rounded bowl and press down so that no pockets of air remain. Place the bowl in the cold part of the refrigerator for an hour. § Wash and dry the celery and chop into sticks about 3 inches long and ¼-inch wide. § Invert the bowl with the cheese onto a serving dish. Press pieces of celery into the cheese all over, so that they stick out like a porcupine's quills. § Serve cold.

■ INGREDIENTS

- ¼ cup butter
- 14 ounces gorgonzola cheese
- 2 tablespoons extra-virgin olive oil
- 12 large stalks celery
- juice of 1 lemon
- freshly ground white pepper

Wine: a dry white (Fiano di Avellino)

Right:
Ricci di gorgonzola e sedano

INGREDIENTS

- 10 ounces spring carrots
- 10 ounces mascarpone cheese
- salt and freshly ground black pepper
- 4 slices *bruschetta* (see recipe p. 16)
- sprigs of parsley, to garnish

Wine: a dry white (Pinot Bianco)

BRUSCHETTE DI CAROTINE AL MASCARPONE
Bruschette with spring carrots and mascarpone cheese

Use the small, sweet carrots that appear in the markets in spring. The cheese and carrot mixture is also good as a snack spread on crackers, toast, or crunchy fresh bread.

Serves 4; Preparation: 10 minutes; Level of difficulty: Simple

Wash the carrots thoroughly. § Grate them into a bowl and add the mascarpone, salt and pepper. Mix well. § Prepare the *bruschetta* and spread the mixture on the slices. § Garnish with the sprigs of parsley and serve.

PALLINE DI CAPRINO E FRUTTA
Caprino cheese and fruit salad

■ INGREDIENTS

- 5 ounces soft caprino cheese
- 4 tablespoons finely chopped fresh herbs (for example – parsley, chives, mint, thyme, marjoram, tarragon, dill, basil)
- 1 small canteloupe, weighing about 12 ounces
- 1 cucumber, peeled
- 4 tablespoons extra-virgin olive oil
- 5 ounces purple grapes
- juice of 1 orange
- salt and freshly ground black pepper
- 12 cherry tomatoes
- 6 small radishes
- fresh spinach or grape leaves

Wine: a semisweet sparkling white (Moscato d'Asti Spumante)

Serves 6; Preparation: 25 minutes; Level of difficulty: Simple

Use your hands to form the caprino into marble-size balls. Roll them in a dish filled with the chopped herbs until they are well coated. Set aside. § Use a small melon baller to make small balls from the canteloupe and cucumber. § Sprinkle the canteloupe balls with 1 tablespoon of orange juice and dust with the black pepper. § Drizzle the cucumber balls with salt and 1 tablespoon of oil. § Wash, dry, and remove the stem from the tomatoes. § Wash, dry, and trim the radishes, cutting off roots and leaves. § Wash and dry the grapes (you can peel them if you like). § Line a large serving bowl with grape leaves or fresh spinach leaves. § Arrange the cheese, vegetables and fruit on top. § Drizzle with the remaining oil and orange juice just before serving.

INSALATA DI PECORINO PERE E NOCI
Pecorino cheese, pear and walnut salad

■ INGREDIENTS

- 8 ounces pecorino romano cheese
- 2 large eating pears
- 6 ounces walnuts
- 1 bunch watercress
- 12 fresh spinach leaves
- 3 tablespoons extra-virgin olive oil
- juice of 1 small lemon
- salt and freshly ground black pepper
- 1 clove garlic, bruised

Wine: a dry or medium, slightly sparkling red (Freisa)

Serves 4-6; Preparation: 15 minutes; Level of difficulty: Simple

Chop the pecorino into ½-inch dice. § Wash, peel and core the pears. Chop into ½-inch dice. § Shell the walnuts and chop coarsely. § Wash and dry the watercress. § Arrange the dark green spinach leaves in the bottom of a salad bowl and add the pears, cheese, watercress, and walnuts. § Put the oil, lemon juice, salt, pepper, and garlic in a small jar. Screw the top down and shake vigorously for 2-3 minutes. When the dressing is well mixed, remove the garlic and drizzle over the salad. § Toss carefully, without disturbing the spinach leaves, and serve.

VARIATION
– Sprinkle ½ cup pitted and chopped black olives over the salad just before tossing.

Left: Palline di caprino e frutta

Uova delle fate
Eggs fairy-style

These colorful eggs are perfect for a children's party. Served with a cool dry white wine, they also make an eyecatching appetizer for an adult or family meal.

Serves 4-6; Preparation: 20 minutes + 30 minutes in the refrigerator; Level of difficulty: Simple

Peel the hard-cooked eggs. Rinse under cold running water to remove any remaining pieces of shell and pat dry with paper towels. Cut a slice off the bottom of each egg so it will stand upright. § Prepare the mayonnaise and spread it over the bottom of a serving dish. Set the eggs, upright, in the mayonnaise, not too close to each other. § Cut the plum tomatoes in half, remove the pulp and seeds, and use the halves to put a "hat" on each upright egg. § Dot the tomato caps with lemon mayonnaise, squeezed from the tube, to look like the spots on mushrooms. § Sprinkle the parsley over the mayonnaise so that it looks like grass. § Garnish with the pieces of bell pepper and gherkin to look like flowers. § Place in the refrigerator for 30 minutes before serving.

■ INGREDIENTS
- 6 hard-cooked eggs
- 1 quantity mayonnaise (see recipe p. 16) + 1 tube lemon mayonnaise
- 3 red plum tomatoes
- 6 tablespoons finely chopped parsley
- ¼ red bell pepper and ¼ yellow bell pepper, cut in tiny diamond shapes
- 6 gherkins, sliced

Wine: a dry, slightly sparkling white (Galestro)

Ricotta alle erbe
Ricotta with herbs

This recipe comes from Trentino-Alto Adige in northeastern Italy. Its delicate flavor calls for the finest quality, freshest ricotta available. When the cheese and herbs are well mixed, store in the refrigerator for about an hour before serving so that the flavor of the herbs will have time to penetrate.

Serves 6; Preparation: 10 minutes + 1 hour in the refrigerator; Level of difficulty: Simple

Combine the ricotta, basil, and parsley in a bowl and mix well. § Add the bay leaves, fennel, salt and pepper, and mix again. § Place in the refrigerator. § Remove the bay leaves and garnish with sprigs of parsley. § Serve cold.

■ INGREDIENTS
- 14 ounces ricotta cheese
- 2 tablespoons finely chopped basil
- 2 tablespoons finely chopped parsley + sprigs to garnish
- 2 bay leaves
- 1 teaspoon fennel seeds
- salt and freshly ground black pepper

Wine: a dry white (Sauvignon)

VARIATION
- Replace the basil with the same amount of finely chopped fresh mint.

Right:
Uova delle fate

Bigné al parmigiano
Parmesan puffs

■ INGREDIENTS

• ⅔ cup cold water

• 3 tablespoons butter

• 1 cup self-raising flour, plus 2 tablespoons for dusting the baking sheet

• salt

• ½ cup freshly grated parmesan cheese

• dash of paprika

• ½ cup sweet almonds

• 2 eggs

Wine: a dry sparkling white (Prosecco)

Serves 4; Preparation: 10 minutes; Cooking: 30 minutes; Level of difficulty: Medium

Put the water in a small saucepan with 2 tablespoons of softened butter over medium heat. § When the water starts to boil, remove the pan from the heat and incorporate the sifted flour and a dash of salt, stirring constantly with a wooden spoon. § Return the saucepan to the heat and cook until the dough is thick, mixing all the time. § Remove from the heat and stir in the parmesan and a dash of paprika. Set aside to cool. § To blanch and peel the almonds, place them in a bowl and pour boiling water over the top so they are barely covered. Leave for 1 minute. Drain and rinse under cold water. Pat dry and slip off the skins. § Chop the almonds finely. § Add the eggs to the dough one at a time. Don't add the second until the first has been thoroughly incorporated. § Beat the dough vigorously. Transfer to a pastry bag with a smooth tube about ¼-inch in diameter. § Butter a baking sheet and dust with flour. § Place marble-size balls of dough on the baking sheet and sprinkle with the almonds, making sure they stick to the puffs. § Bake in a preheated oven at 425°F for 15-20 minutes. The puffs will swell as they bake and dry. § Serve cool.

Pizzette semplici
Little pizzas with tomato, onion and mozzarella cheese

■ INGREDIENTS

BASE

• 1 ounce active dry yeast

• about 1 cup warm water

• 4 cups all-purpose flour

• 2 tablespoons extra-virgin olive oil

• salt

Serves 4; Preparation: 10 minutes + 2 hours resting; Cooking: 25-30 minutes; Level of difficulty: Simple

In a small bowl gently stir the yeast into half the warm water. Set aside to rest for 10 minutes. § Sift a quarter of the flour into a large bowl and make a well in the center. Add the olive oil. § Gradually stir in the water and yeast and the flour, adding as much of the remaining water as necessary to obtain a smooth, firm dough. § Add 2 pinches of salt. § Turn the dough out onto a clean, lightly floured counter. Form it into a ball and then knead and fold

Right:

Pizzette semplici

TOPPING

- 1 14-ounce can peeled and chopped tomatoes
- 1 tablespoon capers
- 1 clove garlic, finely chopped
- generous dash oregano
- salt and freshly ground black pepper
- 5 ounces mozzarella cheese, diced

Wine: a light, dry red (Vino Novello)

until a smooth, elastic dough has been obtained. § Sprinkle with flour and wrap the dough in a clean tea towel. Place in a warm spot in the kitchen (or wrap in a woolen garment) and leave to rise until it has doubled in size. This will take about 1½-2 hours. § Mix the tomatoes, capers, garlic, oregano, salt and pepper together in a bowl. § Oil a baking sheet. § Break the dough into four pieces and, using kneading movements, press each one out to form a small round pizza. § Distribute the tomato mixture evenly over the top of each. § Bake in a preheated oven at 400°F for 20-25 minutes. § Remove from the oven and sprinkle with the mozzarella. Return to the oven for about 5 minutes, or until the mozzarella has melted and browned a little. § Take the pizzas out of the oven and serve hot or cold.

CREMA DI UOVA E PEPERONI
Egg and bell pepper cream

Egg and bell pepper cream makes a refreshing and unusual antipasto *for summer dinner parties. However, I strongly recommend that you try it out a few times before the invitations go out. A lot depends on the quantity of water the bell peppers produce during cooking and the size of the eggs. You really must make the dish a couple of times and learn for yourself how to adjust the ingredients to suit each time. Good luck!*

Serves 4-6; Preparation: 50 minutes + 2 hours in the refrigerator; Cooking: 30 minutes; Level of difficulty: Complicated

Wash the bell peppers, dry, and remove the seeds and cores. Cut into small pieces, keeping the colors separate. § Place 2 tablespoons of oil in three separate saucepans, divide the onion in three parts, and sauté a part in each. § When the onion is transparent, add salt, pepper, 2 tablespoons of water, and bell peppers, keeping the colors separate in each pan. § Cover each pan and cook over medium heat for about 30 minutes, or until the bell peppers are soft and well-cooked. § Remove the pans from the heat and let the mixtures cool. § Blend the contents of each pan separately in a food processor until a smooth purée. § Soften the gelatin in a little water. § Heat the milk in a pot, but don't let it boil. § Beat the egg yolks in a bowl and add the hot milk a bit at a time, stirring continuously. Season with salt and pepper. § Transfer to a saucepan and heat to just below boiling point, stirring frequently. Add the gelatin. § Remove from the heat and beat with a fork so that the gelatin dissolves. § Pour equal parts of the mixture into three different bowls and let cool. § Add one color of bell pepper purée to each and stir. § Whip the cream to stiff peaks and fold in equal parts to each of the three bowls. § Moisten a rectangular mold with water and pour in the yellow mixture. Place the mold in the refrigerator for 10 minutes. § Remove and pour in the red mixture. Return the mold to the refrigerator for 10 more minutes. § Remove again and add the green mixture. § Refrigerate for at least 2 hours. § Just before serving, dip the mold for a second in hot water and invert the cream on a serving dish.

Right:
Crema di uova e peperoni

CRÊPES AI QUATTRO FORMAGGI
Crêpes with four-cheese filling

Serves 6; Preparation: 20 minutes + 1 hour for the crêpes; Cooking: 20 minutes; Level of difficulty: Medium

Beat the eggs in a bowl with a fork or whisk. § Sift the flour and salt into another bowl and stir the milk in gradually so that no lumps form. When it is smooth, pour it into the eggs. § Beat vigorously, then cover the bowl with plastic wrap and let stand in the coldest part of the refrigerator for about 40-50 minutes. § Before using, beat again for a few seconds. § Set a crêpe pan on the heat and grease well. Use a small ladle to pour 1-2 scoops of batter into the pan. Rotate the pan so that the batter covers the bottom evenly. § When the crêpe has set, turn it over using a spatula, your hands, or by flipping it. § When golden on both sides, slide it onto a plate. § Keep making crêpes until the batter is finished. Remember to grease the pan for each new crêpe. § Prepare the béchamel sauce. § Add half the parmesan, the gruyère, fontina, and gorgonzola to the béchamel. Cook over low heat until the cheeses have blended in with the sauce. § Spread 2-3 tablespoons of the cheese mixture on each crêpe. Roll the crêpes up and place them in a lightly buttered ovenproof dish. § Cover with the remaining cheese sauce and sprinkle with the remaining parmesan. Grind a little black pepper over the top and add several tiny knobs of butter. § Bake in a preheated oven at 350°F for 15 minutes, or until the topping is golden brown. § Serve piping hot straight from the oven.

■ INGREDIENTS

- 3 eggs
- ¾ cup all-purpose flour
- 1½ cups milk
- ¼ cup butter, to grease the crêpe pan
- 1 quantity béchamel (see recipe p. 20)
- salt and freshly ground black pepper
- generous ½ cup freshly grated parmesan cheese
- generous ½ cup freshly grated gruyère cheese
- generous ½ cup diced fontina cheese
- generous ½ cup diced gorgonzola cheese

Wine: a young, dry red (Roero)

BOMBOLINE DI PARMIGIANO
Fried parmesan puffs

Serves 6; Preparation: 20 minutes; Cooking: 20 minutes; Level of difficulty: Medium

Combine the water with the salt and butter in a saucepan and bring to a boil. § Add the sifted flour all at once, remove from the heat, and stir vigorously with a wooden spoon. § When the mixture is smooth, return to the heat and cook till the batter pulls away from the sides of the pan. Set aside to cool. § Add the eggs one at a time and mix each one in before adding the next. § Add the cheeses and nutmeg. § Mold the mixture into marble-size balls. § Heat the oil in a deep-sided skillet until very hot and fry the puffs a few at a time until golden brown. § Place on paper towels to drain, sprinkle with salt, and serve hot.

■ INGREDIENTS

- scant 1 cup water
- 1 teaspoon salt
- 3 tablespoons butter
- 1 cup all-purpose flour
- 4 eggs
- 1 cup freshly grated parmesan cheese
- ½ cup grated emmenthal cheese
- dash of nutmeg
- oil, for frying

Wine: a dry red (Grignolino)

Right: *Crêpes ai quattro formaggi*

■ INGREDIENTS

- 1 onion, finely chopped
- 4 tablespoons extra-virgin olive oil
- 1¾ cups canned tomatoes
- 6 leaves fresh basil, torn
- 1 teaspoon dried oregano
- salt
- 4 slices plain or wholewheat bread
- 5 ounces mozzarella cheese, thinly sliced

Wine: a dry rosé (Lizzano)

CROSTINI PUGLIESI
Mozzarella crostini Puglia-style

Serves 4; Preparation: 15 minutes; Cooking: 45 minutes; Level of difficulty: Simple

Sauté the onion in half the oil until transparent. § Add the tomatoes, basil, half the oregano, and salt, and simmer for 30 minutes. § Cut the slices of bread in half, cover with the mozzarella, and place in an oiled baking dish. Sprinkle with the remaining oregano, drizzle with the rest of the oil, and bake in a preheated oven at 400°F until the bread is crisp and the mozzarella melted. § Remove from the oven and spread with the tomato sauce. § Serve hot.

Malfatti di parmigiano e spinaci
Parmesan and spinach dumplings

Malfatti in Italian means "badly made" and refers to the fact that these little dumplings are similar to the stuffing used for ravioli. They are badly made because they lack their pasta wrappings. In Tuscany they are sometimes called Strozzaprete, *or "priest chokers," although the origin of this name remains obscure.*

Serves 6; Preparation: 20 minutes; Cooking: 20 minutes; Level of difficulty: Medium

Cook the spinach in a pot of salted, boiling water until tender (3-4 minutes if frozen, 8-10 minutes if fresh). Drain well and squeeze out excess moisture. Chop finely. § Mix the spinach with the ricotta, eggs, parmesan (reserving 2 tablespoons), and nutmeg. Season with salt and pepper. § Mold the mixture into walnut-sized balls. § Bring a large pot of salted water to a boil, add the dumplings, and cook until they rise to the surface. § Remove with a slotted spoon and place in a serving dish. § Melt the butter and sage together, season with salt and pepper, and pour over the dumplings. § Sprinkle with the remaining parmesan and serve hot.

> ### Variation
> – The dumplings make a delicious winter *antipasto* when baked. When the dumplings are cooked, drain well and place them in an ovenproof baking dish. Pour the melted butter and sage sauce over the top (or replace with 1 quantity Basic tomato sauce—see recipe p. 22). Sprinkle with ½ cup freshly grated parmesan and bake in a preheated oven at 350°F for about 15 minutes, or until the topping is golden brown.

Fritta di mozzarella e polenta
Fried mozzarella and polenta cubes

This is a good way to use up leftover polenta.

Serves 6; Preparation: 10 minutes; Cooking: 15 minutes; Level of difficulty: Simple

Chop the polenta and the mozzarella into cubes about 1 inch square. § Grind the pepper over the mozzarella. § Place a cube of mozzarella between two cubes of polenta and thread them together with a wooden toothpick. § Heat the oil in a deep-sided skillet until very hot. § Cook the polenta and cheese cubes until they turn golden. § Drain on paper towels, sprinkle with a little salt, and serve immediately.

■ INGREDIENTS

- 1½ pounds fresh or 1 pound frozen spinach
- 5 ounces ricotta
- 1 egg and 1 yolk
- 1 cup freshly grated parmesan cheese
- dash of nutmeg
- salt and freshly ground black pepper
- 2 tablespoons butter
- 5 fresh sage leaves, torn

Wine: a young, dry red (Vino Novello)

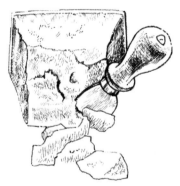

■ INGREDIENTS

- ½ quantity cold polenta (see recipe p. 18), sliced
- 6 ounces mozzarella cheese
- freshly ground white pepper
- 2 cups oil, for frying

Wine: a dry red (Chianti)

Right:
Malfatti di parmigiano e spinaci

ROTOLONE D'UOVO
Omelet roll

■ INGREDIENTS

- 6 eggs
- 1 tablespoon all-purpose flour
- 1 tablespoon freshly grated parmesan
- 2 tablespoons milk
- salt
- 2 tablespoons butter
- ½ quantity mayonnaise (see recipe p. 16)
- 1 tablespoon mustard
- 6 gherkins, finely chopped
- 3½ ounces ham, sliced
- 3 ounces mortadella, in a single thick slice
- 8 radishes, chopped
- 1 cucumber, finely sliced

Serves 6; Preparation: 20 minutes + 4 hours in the refrigerator; Cooking: 20 minutes; Level of difficulty: Medium

In a bowl whisk the eggs with the flour, parmesan, milk, and salt. § Melt the butter in a skillet and pour in the egg mixture. Cook until golden on one side, then flip and cook on the other. § Drain on paper towels and set aside to cool. § Prepare the mayonnaise and mix with the mustard and gherkins. § Arrange the ham on the omelet and spread with a layer of mayonnaise. Cover with the mortadella and roll the omelet up, being careful not to break it. § Wrap in aluminum foil and keep in the refrigerator for at least 4 hours. § Just before serving, cut the roll in slices and arrange on a serving dish. Garnish with radishes and cucumber.

Wine: a dry red (Merlot dell'Isonzo)

PARMIGIANA DI ZUCCHINE
Zucchini and parmesan pie

■ INGREDIENTS

- 1½ pounds zucchini
- 2 cups oil, for frying
- 2 cloves garlic
- 1 onion, finely chopped
- 1¾ cups peeled and chopped fresh or canned tomatoes
- 8 fresh basil leaves, torn
- salt and freshly ground black pepper
- 1 tablespoon extra-virgin olive oil
- 12 tablespoons freshly grated parmesan cheese
- 6½ ounces mozzarella cheese, in thin slices
- 1 tablespoon butter

Serves 6; Preparation: 20 minutes; Cooking: 35 minutes; Level of difficulty: Simple

Wash the zucchini and trim the ends. Slice lengthwise in ¼-inch strips. § Heat the frying oil in a skillet and cook the zucchini for about 10 minutes, or until they are golden brown. § Drain well on paper towels and set aside in the warming oven. § Sauté the garlic and onion over medium heat in a skillet with the olive oil. § Remove the garlic and add the tomatoes, basil, and salt. Cook for 10 minutes, stirring from time to time with a wooden spoon. § Grease an ovenproof dish with a little olive oil and cover the bottom with a layer of tomato sauce. Add a layer of zucchini slices, another of tomato sauce, sprinkle with parmesan, and cover with a layer of mozzarella slices. Repeat until all the ingredients are used up, leaving a little mozzarella and parmesan for the topping. § Arrange knobs of butter and grind a little black pepper over the top. § Bake in a preheated oven at 350°F for 15 minutes, or until the topping is golden brown.

Wine: a dry red (Elba rosso)

Right: *Parmigiana di zucchine*

Sformatini di semolino
Semolina molds

Serves 4; Preparation: 15 minutes + 2 hours for the meat sauce; Cooking: 30 minutes; Level of difficulty: Simple

Prepare the meat sauce. § Add a dash of salt to the milk and bring to a boil. § As the milk begins to boil, sift in the semolina, stirring constantly. Cook for about 10 minutes over low heat, stirring all the time. § Remove from the heat and add the nutmeg, half the butter, the parmesan, and 2 egg yolks. § Butter four pudding molds 4 inches in diameter and sprinkle with bread crumbs. Line the sides and the bottom with the semolina mixture. § Put a piece of fontina and 1 tablespoon of meat sauce in the center of each one, then fill completely with semolina. § Bake in a preheated oven at 400°F for 15-20 minutes. § When cooked, remove from the oven and invert into a casserole. § Return to the oven for a few minutes so they will brown. § Serve hot with the remaining sauce.

■ INGREDIENTS

• 1 quantity meat sauce (see recipe p. 22)
• salt and freshly ground black pepper
• 3 cups milk
• 1 cup semolina
• dash of nutmeg
• scant ½ cup butter
• ¼ cup freshly grated parmesan cheese
• 2 egg yolks
• 3½ ounces fontina cheese
• 2 tablespoons bread crumbs

Wine: a dry red (Barolo)

Frittata di menta
Mint omelet

Serves 6; Preparation: 10 minutes; Cooking: 10 minutes; Level of difficulty: Simple

Beat the eggs in a bowl until foamy, then add the bread crumbs, pecorino, mint, parsley, and a dash of pepper and salt. § Heat the oil in a deep-sided skillet until very hot. § Pour in the egg mixture. Spread it out over the bottom and cook over medium heat until the underside turns golden brown. § Flip the omelet with the help of a lid or plate. Don't let it cook too much; a good *frittata* is supposed to be fairly soft. § Serve hot.

■ INGREDIENTS

• 6 eggs
• ½ cup bread crumbs
• 1¼ cups freshly grated pecorino cheese
• 12 fresh mint leaves, finely chopped
• 2 tablespoons finely chopped parsley
• salt and freshly ground black pepper
• 4 tablespoons extra-virgin olive oil

Wine: a dry white (Bianco di Pitigliano)

VARIATION
– For a completely different but equally delicious dish, replace the mint with 9 ounces of fresh cauliflower florets. The cauliflower should be sautéed for 8-10 minutes in the oil before adding the egg mixture. Zucchini are also good when prepared in this way.

Right:
Sformatini di semolino

- 14 ounces tasty provolone cheese
- 4 tablespoons extra-virgin olive oil
- 1 clove garlic, cut in two
- 1 tablespoon white wine vinegar
- 1 teaspoon oregano
- ½ teaspoon sugar

Wine: a dry red (Cirò)

CACIU ALL'ARGINTERA
Sweet and sour fried cheese

*This simple and tasty dish comes from Sicily, in the south.
Provolone is a hard cheese and will not melt during cooking.*

Serves 4; Preparation: 5 minutes; Cooking: 15 minutes; Level of difficulty: Simple

Cut the cheese in slices about ¼-inch thick. § Heat the oil and the garlic in a skillet. As soon as it is hot, put in the slices of cheese and brown on both sides. § When they are uniformly browned, sprinkle with the vinegar and dust with the oregano and sugar. § Serve immediately.

CROSTATA DI FORMAGGIO ALLO ZAFFERANO
Saffron cheese pie

Serves 6; Preparation: 20 minutes + 1 hour in the refrigerator; Cooking: 45 minutes; Level of difficulty: Simple

Prepare the dough: mix the flour with the butter (set aside a knob), oil, salt, 1 whole egg and 1 yolk. Do not overmix as the dough could become hard. § Wrap in a sheet of waxed paper and place in the refrigerator for an hour. § For the filling: put the ricotta in a bowl and mash with a fork. Add the gruyère, softened butter, saffron and, one at a time, the egg yolks, mixing well. § Beat the egg whites until stiff and fold into the mixture. § Roll out the dough and line a buttered pie pan. § Fill with the cheese mixture. § Bake the pie in a preheated oven at 350°F for 45 minutes. § Serve hot or cold.

■ INGREDIENTS

DOUGH
- 4 cups all-purpose flour
- 5 tablespoons butter, softened and chopped
- 2 tablespoons extra-virgin olive oil
- salt
- 1 egg and 1 yolk

FILLING
- 14 ounces ricotta cheese
- 1¼ cups grated gruyère cheese
- scant ½ cup butter
- generous dash of saffron
- 6 eggs, separated

Wine: a dry white (Frascati)

TORTELLI DI FORMAGGIO
Cheese tortelli

Serves 6; Preparation: 20 minutes; Cooking: 20 minutes; Level of difficulty: Simple

Put the two cheeses, flour, parsley, fennel seeds, and nutmeg in a bowl. Add 3 of the eggs and half the bread crumbs and mix well. § Beat the remaining egg with a fork in a shallow dish. Season with salt and pepper. § Shape walnut-sized balls with the cheese mixture, dusting your hands with flour to facilitate the process. § Dip the balls first in the beaten egg, and then in the remaining bread crumbs. § Melt the butter in a skillet, add the tortelli, and fry until golden brown. Drain on paper towels. § Transfer to a serving dish, sprinkle with salt, and serve hot.

■ INGREDIENTS

- 1½ cups grated gruyère cheese
- ¾ cup freshly grated parmesan cheese
- 2 tablespoons all-purpose flour
- 1 tablespoon finely chopped parsley
- dash of fennel seeds
- dash of nutmeg
- 4 eggs
- 1½ cups bread crumbs
- salt and freshly ground mixed pepper
- 2 tablespoons butter

Wine: a dry red (Dolcetto)

Right: *Crostata di formaggio allo zafferano*

BOCCONCINI DI FORMAGGIO E PROSCIUTTO
Ham and cheese tidbits

Serves 4-6; Preparation: 10 minutes + 30 minutes resting; Cooking: 20 minutes; Level of difficulty: Simple

Mix the flour with the softened butter, 2 eggs, and a dash of salt. If necessary, add a little water and knead until the dough is smooth. § Wrap the dough in a cloth and set aside in a cool place for 30 minutes. § Roll out the dough in a thin sheet and cut into rectangles. § Cut the slices of ham and fontina to the same size as the pieces of dough. § Place pieces of ham, fontina, and anchovy on half the pieces of dough, cover with the remaining dough and press the edges together to seal. § Beat the remaining egg and brush the tops with it. § Place the tidbits on a buttered baking sheet and bake in a preheated oven at 350°F for 25 minutes, or until golden brown. § Serve hot.

■ INGREDIENTS

- 2½ cups all-purpose flour
- ⅔ cup butter
- 3 eggs
- salt
- 10 ounces ham, cut in thick slices
- 5 ounces fontina, sliced
- 8 anchovy fillets, crumbled

Wine: a dry, sparkling red (Lambrusco di Sorbara)

INSALATA DI UOVO, PROVOLONE, MELE E RADICCHIO ROSSO
Egg, provolone, apple, and radicchio salad

Serves 4-6; Preparation: 15 minutes + 1 hour for the radicchio rosso; Level of difficulty: Simple

To clean the radicchio rosso, discard the outer leaves, wash several times, dry well and place in the bottom of a salad bowl. § Season with the lemon juice and half the oil, toss well and set aside for about an hour. § Slice the eggs with an egg cutter. § Peel the apples and dice. § Cut the provolone into cubes. § Add the eggs, apples, provolone, and olives to the salad bowl. § Mix the mustard, vinegar, remaining oil, salt and pepper together in a bowl. Beat vigorously with a fork and pour over the salad. § Toss well and serve.

■ INGREDIENTS

- 10 ounces radicchio rosso
- juice of 1 small lemon
- 6 tablespoons extra-virgin olive oil
- 3 hard-cooked eggs
- 3 crisp eating apples
- 6 ounces provolone cheese
- 16 pitted and chopped large black olives
- 2 tablespoons hot mustard
- 1 tablespoon white wine vinegar
- salt and freshly ground black pepper

Wine: a dry white (Galestro)

Right: *Insalata di uovo, provolone, mele e radicchio rosso*

VARIATIONS
– Add a few chopped walnuts to give extra flavor to the salad.
– Replace the radicchio rosso with the same quantity of fresh spinach.

BARCHETTE DI FORMAGGIO
Cheese-filled barchette

*A simple creamy cheese and béchamel filling highlights the delicate flavor of the pastry.
Experiment with mixes of your favorite cheeses.*

Serves 4-6; Preparation: 20 minutes + time to make the barchette; Cooking: 20 minutes; Level of difficulty: Simple
Prepare the *barchette*. § Make a thick béchamel sauce. § Cut the cheeses
in pieces, add to the béchamel sauce, and stir well over very low heat
until melted. § Fill the *barchette* with the sauce and cook in a preheated
oven at 350°F for a 5-10 minutes to brown. § Serve hot.

■ INGREDIENTI

• 12 *barchette* (see recipe p. 20)
• 1 quantity béchamel sauce (see recipe p. 20)
• 3 ounces emmenthal cheese
• 6½ ounces mozzarella cheese
• 3 ounces fontina cheese

Wine: a dry white (Corvo)

CROCCHETE DI FONTINA
Fontina croquettes

INGREDIENTS

- 3 cups all-purpose flour
- 3 cups buckwheat flour
- ½ cup milk
- 2 cups diced fontina cheese
- ½ cup butter
- dash of nutmeg
- salt and freshly grated black pepper
- 2 eggs (beaten) + 1 yolk
- 1¾ cups bread crumbs
- 2 cups oil, for frying

Wine: a dry red
(Chianti Classico)

This dish is a rather filling antipasto and should be followed by something light.

Serves 6-8; Preparation: 15 minutes; Cooking: 15 minutes; Level of difficulty: Simple

Mix the two types of flour together in a saucepan. Stir in the milk, fontina, butter, nutmeg, salt and pepper. § Cook over low heat for about 20 minutes, stirring continuously until a fairly dense cream forms. § Remove from the heat and add the egg yolk, continuing to stir with a wooden spoon. Pour the mixture into a buttered dish and let cool. § Mold the mixture into small oblong croquettes, dip them in the beaten egg, and roll in the bread crumbs. § Heat the oil in a deep-sided skillet until very hot and fry the croquettes a few at a time until they are golden brown. § Sprinkle with a little salt and serve hot.

MOZZARELLA FRITTA
Fried mozzarella

INGREDIENTS

- 8 ounces mozzarella cheese
- ½ cup all-purpose flour
- 2 eggs
- 1½ cups bread crumbs
- 2 cups oil, for frying
- salt

Wine: a dry red
(San Severo Rosso)

Serves 4; Preparation: 5 minutes; Cooking: 10 minutes; Level of difficulty: Simple

Cut the mozzarella in rather thick slices and cover with flour. § Beat the eggs in a bowl and dip the slices in the egg and then in the bread crumbs. § Heat the oil in a deep-sided skillet until very hot and deep-fry the slices until golden brown on both sides. § Drain on paper towels, sprinkle with salt, and serve piping hot.

MOZZARELLA PICCANTE
Mozzarella and mixed pickled vegetables

INGREDIENTS

- 12 slices tomato
- 12 slices mozzarella
- 1 cup mixed pickled vegetables

Wine: a light, sparkling red
(Lambrusco)

Left:
Barchette di formaggio

Serves 4; Preparation: 10 minutes + 30 minutes in the refrigerator; Level of difficulty: Simple

Place a slice of mozzarella on each slice of tomato. § Purée the pickled vegetables together in a food processor. § Place a spoonful of vegetables on each slice of mozzarella. § Keep in the refrigerator for 30 minutes before serving.

FISH APPETIZERS

Italian seafood cookery is simpler than in most other cuisines. But it relies on the freshest, highest quality ingredients. With the exception of the smoked salmon, tuna fish, and salt cod, all the recipes in this section call for fresh fish. You may try them using frozen fish, but the results will not be as good. Be warned!

Cozze ripiene al forno
Stuffed baked mussels

Serves 6; Preparation: 20 minutes + 1 hour to soak mussels; Cooking: 25 minutes; Level of difficulty: Simple

Soak the mussels in a large bowl of water for at least an hour to purge them of sand. Pull off their beards, scrub, and rinse well in abundant cold water. § Put the mussels in a large skillet over medium-high heat, sprinkle with the wine, and cover. § When all the shells are open (discard any that don't open), remove from the skillet. Discard all the empty half shells, keeping only those with the mussel inside. § Remove the crusts from the rolls and soak the insides in the milk for 10 minutes. Squeeze out excess moisture with your hands. § Combine most of the parsley and garlic in a bowl with the bread. Add 4 tablespoons of grated parmesan cheese, the oil, salt and pepper. Mix well. § Fill the shells with the mixture, then arrange them in a large, greased baking dish. Dust with the remaining parmesan and bake in a preheated oven at 400°F for about 15 minutes. § Just before serving, sprinkle the rest of the garlic and parsley on top, and serve hot.

INGREDIENTS
- 60 mussels in shell
- ½ cup dry white wine
- 3 day-old bread rolls
- 1 cup milk
- 4 tablespoons finely chopped parsley
- 4 cloves garlic, finely chopped
- 6 tablespoons freshly grated parmesan cheese
- 2 tablespoons extra-virgin olive oil
- salt and freshly ground black pepper

Wine: a dry white (Cinqueterre)

Impepata di cozze
Mussels in pepper sauce

*This fiery dish makes a perfect appetizer when followed by oven-roasted fish.
Vary the amount of pepper depending on your tastes.*

Serves 6; Preparation: 10 minutes + 1 hour to soak mussels; Cooking: 10 minutes; Level of difficulty: Simple

Soak the mussels in a large bowl of water for at least an hour to purge them of sand. Pull off their beards, scrub, and rinse well in abundant cold water. § Sauté the parsley and garlic in a skillet with the oil for 4-5 minutes. Season with salt. § Add the mussels and cook over medium heat until they are all open. Discard any that haven't opened. § Add the pepper and cook for 2 minutes more, stirring all the time. § Prepare the *bruschetta* and place a slice in each serving dish. Cover with mussels and spoon some of the sauce from the skillet over each portion. § Serve hot.

INGREDIENTS
- 60 mussels in shell
- 4 tablespoons finely chopped parsley
- 1 clove garlic, finely chopped
- 2 tablespoons extra-virgin olive oil
- salt
- 1 heaping teaspoon freshly ground black pepper
- 6 slices *bruschetta* (see recipe p. 16)

Wine: a dry white (Corvo bianco)

Right: *Impepata di cozze*

Vongole in salsa di panna fresca
Clams in fresh cream sauce

■ INGREDIENTS

- 4 pounds clams in shell
- 1 cup dry white wine
- 1 medium onion, finely chopped
- 2 cloves garlic, finely chopped
- ¼ cup butter
- 2 tablespoons all-purpose flour
- salt and freshly ground black pepper
- 1¼ cups fresh light cream
- 1 egg, beaten
- 1 tablespoon finely chopped parsley
- juice of ½ lemon

Wine: a dry white
(Roero Arneis)

Serves 6; Preparation: 30 minutes + 1 hour to soak the clams; Cooking: 15 minutes; Level of difficulty: Simple

Soak the clams in a large bowl of water for at least an hour to remove any sand. Scrub and rinse well in abundant cold water. § Put them in a skillet with the wine, cover, and cook over medium-high heat. Take the clams out as they open. Arrange them on a serving dish and keep them in a warm place. § Strain the liquid left in the skillet and set aside to cool. § In the same sauté the onion and garlic in the butter until they turn golden. Add the flour and mix rapidly. § Gradually add the strained clam liquid and mix well until you have a thick, creamy sauce. Season with salt and pepper. § Beat the cream, egg, parsley, and lemon juice together and add to the clam sauce. Mix rapidly and then pour over the clams. § Serve at once.

Cozze gratinate al forno
Baked mussels

■ INGREDIENTS

- 2 pounds fresh mussels
- 2 tablespoons finely chopped parsley
- 2 cloves garlic, finely chopped
- 1¾ cups bread crumbs
- 3 tablespoons extra-virgin olive oil
- salt and freshly ground black pepper
- 1 tablespoon butter
- juice of 1 small lemon

Wine: a dry white
(Ischia bianco)

Serves 4; Preparation: 30 minutes+1 hour to soak the mussels; Cooking: 15 minutes; Level of difficulty: Simple

Soak the mussels in a large bowl of water for at least an hour to purge them of sand. Pull off their beards, scrub, and rinse well in abundant cold water. § Transfer to a skillet, cover, and cook over medium-high heat until they are all open. Discard any that haven't opened. § Set the liquid they produce aside. § Mix the parsley and garlic together in a bowl with the bread crumbs, 1 tablespoon of oil, salt and pepper. Strain the mussel liquid and add about 3 tablespoons to the bread mixture. Mix well. § Arrange the mussels in a buttered ovenproof dish. Fill each one with some of the mixture and drizzle with the remaining oil and lemon juice. § Bake in a preheated oven at 400°F for 15-20 minutes, or until the bread crumbs turn golden brown. § Serve hot.

Right: Vongole in salsa di panna fresca

- 14 ounces dried salt cod (skinned and boned)
- 1 cup all-purpose flour
- ½ cup warm water
- 1 tablespoon extra-virgin olive oil
- salt
- 2 cups oil, for frying

Wine: a dry white
(Colli di Luni bianco)

FRITTELLE DI BACCALÀ
Salt cod fritters

When buying salt cod, always choose meaty, cream-colored fillets. Avoid the brown ones.

Serves 4; Preparation: 15 minutes + 24 hours to soak cod; Cooking: 20 minutes; Level of difficulty: Simple

Put the salt cod in a bowl of cold water to soak a day ahead. § In a bowl combine the flour and enough of the water to obtain a thick batter. Add the olive oil, season with salt, and stir continuously for 5 minutes. § Wash the salt cod in running water, dry, and cut in pieces. § Heat the oil to very hot in a deep-sided skillet, dip the pieces of salt cod in the batter, and deep-fry until golden brown. § Drain on paper towels, sprinkle with salt, and serve hot.

Calamari dolci delicati
Filled sweet squid

■ INGREDIENTS

- 2 pounds small squid
- 1 small onion, finely chopped
- 1 cup muscatel raisins
- ⅔ cup pine nuts
- 1¾ cups bread crumbs
- 2 eggs, beaten to a foam
- salt and freshly ground white pepper
- 2 tablespoons extra-virgin olive oil
- 1 cup white wine

Wine: a dry white
(Verdicchio dei Castelli di Jesi)

Serves 4; Preparation: 30 minutes; Cooking: 30 minutes; Level of difficulty: Simple

Choose small squid that are all about the same size. § To clean the squid, separate the tentacles and head from the body by grasping the head and pulling it apart from the body. Remove the ink sac from the head. Peel off the skin. Remove the bony part and clean out the insides. Rinse well in cold running water. § Cut off the tentacles and blanch the bodies in boiling water for 2-3 minutes. Set aside to cool. § Chop the tentacles in small pieces and put them in a bowl with the onion, raisins, pine nuts, bread crumbs, and egg. Mix well and season with salt and pepper. § Fill the squid bodies with the mixture and close them with a toothpick so the filling won't come out during cooking. § Heat the oil in a heavy-bottomed pan (or an earthenware pot), add the filled squid, and cook slowly over medium-low heat. Turn them often so they won't stick to the bottom. § After about 15 minutes, add the white wine and continue cooking until the liquid has evaporated. § Serve hot.

Spiedini di scampi
Skewered grilled shrimp

■ INGREDIENTS

- 2 pounds giant shrimp
- 4 tablespoons all-purpose flour
- scant ½ cup fresh butter
- salt and freshly ground black pepper
- 1 lemon and sprigs of parsley, to garnish

Wine: a dry white
(Sauvignon del Collio)

This recipe calls for a grill pan to place over the element on a gas or electric stove (see Utensils pp. 14-15) to cook the shrimp. They are also very good if cooked over a barbecue, from which they will take a delicious smokey flavor.

Serves 6; Preparation: 30 minutes; Cooking: 30 minutes; Level of difficulty: Simple

Shell the shrimp and remove the dark intestinal veins. Chop off the heads and rinse thoroughly in cold running water. § Thread the shrimp onto skewers and sprinkle with the flour. § Melt the butter in a saucepan and pour half of it over the shrimp. Sprinkle with salt and pepper. § Heat the grill pan to very hot and place the skewers in it. Let the shrimp cook on one side before turning to cook on the other. § Lay the skewers on a serving dish, garnish with lemon and parsley, and serve hot. The remaining melted butter should be served separately in a warmed dish.

Right:
Calamari dolci delicati

Conchiglie di Pesce
Scallop shells filled with fish, potato and mayonnaise

This tasty fish appetizer is easy to make and can be prepared ahead of time. Ask your fish vendor for scallop shells or serve the fish mixture in the curved inner leaves of lettuce hearts.

Serves 4; Preparation: 15 minutes; Cooking: 40 minutes; Level of difficulty: Simple

Prepare the mayonnaise. § Chop the boiled fish and mix with the diced potatoes. § Add the parsley, capers, mayonnaise, salt and pepper. Mix carefully. § Spoon the mixture into the scallop shells and set aside in a cool place for 30 minutes before serving. Garnish with slices of lemon and sprigs of parsley.

■ INGREDIENTS

- ½ quantity mayonnaise (see recipe p. 16)
- 14 ounces boiled fish fillets (hake, sea bream, sea bass, or other)
- 3 boiled potatoes, peeled
- 1 tablespoon finely chopped parsley
- 1 tablespoon capers
- salt and black pepper
- lemon and sprigs of parsley, to garnish

Wine: a dry white (Verduzzo Friulano)

Insalata di Mare
Seafood salad

Serves 8; Preparation: 1 hour + 30 minutes in refrigerator; Cooking: 30 minutes; Level of difficulty: Medium

Clean the squid and separate the tentacles and head from the body by grasping the head and pulling it apart from the body. Remove the ink sac from the head. Remove the bony part and clean out the insides. § To clean the cuttlefish, cut each one lengthwise and remove the internal bone and the stomach. Discard the internal ink sac. § Place the cuttlefish in a pot with 5 quarts of cold water and 1 tablespoon of salt and bring to a boil over high heat. § When the cuttlefish have been simmering for 5 minutes, add the squid and cook for 15 more minutes. § Drain and set aside to cool. § Chop the tentacles in small pieces and then slice the bodies in rings. Transfer to a salad bowl. § Bring 6 cups of water and 1 tablespoon of salt to a boil. Rinse the shrimp thoroughly and add to the pot. Cook for 2 minutes. Drain and set aside to cool. § Shell the shrimp and add them to the salad bowl. § Soak the clams and mussels in a large bowl of water for at least an hour. Pull the beards off the mussels. Scrub well and rinse in abundant cold water. § Place the shellfish in a large skillet with 2 tablespoons of oil and cook over medium heat until they are all open. Discard any that have not opened. § Discard the shells and add the mussels and clams to the salad bowl. § Mix the parsley, garlic, chilies, lemon juice, remaining oil, salt and pepper in a bowl. Pour over the salad and toss well. § Place in the refrigerator for 30 minutes before serving.

■ INGREDIENTS

- 1 pound squid
- 14 ounces cuttlefish
- salt
- 14 ounces shrimp
- 14 ounces clams in shell
- 14 ounces mussels in shell
- 2 tablespoons finely chopped parsley
- 2 cloves garlic, finely chopped
- 1 teaspoon crushed chilies (optional)
- juice of ½ lemon
- 5 tablespoons extra-virgin olive oil
- freshly ground black pepper

Wine: a dry white (Greco di Tufo)

Right: *Insalata di mare*

MOUSSE DI TONNO
Tuna fish mousse

■ INGREDIENTS

- 8 ounces tuna fish in oil
- 8 ounces mascarpone cheese
- 2 ounces pickled onions, well drained and very finely chopped
- 1 tablespoon finely chopped parsley
- salt and freshly ground black pepper
- 1 tablespoon butter
- 1 bunch arugula (rocket)
- 8 black olives, pitted and chopped

Wine: a dry white (Locorotondo)

Serves 4; Preparation: 15 minutes + 6 hours in the refrigerator; Level of difficulty: Simple
Put the tuna fish in the food processor and whizz for 1-2 minutes. § Transfer to a bowl and add the mascarpone. Mix well and add the pickled onions and parsley. Season with salt and pepper. § Lightly butter a mold and line with aluminum foil. Fill with the tuna mixture and place in the refrigerator for 6 hours. § Wash and dry the arugula and arrange on a serving dish. Invert the mousse onto the bed of arugula. § Garnish with the olives and serve.

BIGNOLINE DI COZZE
Mussel dumplings

■ INGREDIENTS

- 1½ pounds mussels in shell
- ½ cup dry white wine
- ¾ cup cold water
- 2 tablespoons butter
- salt
- 3½ ounces all-purpose flour
- 4 eggs
- 2 tablespoons finely chopped parsley
- 4 tablespoons freshly grated parmesan cheese
- 2 cups oil, for frying

Wine: a dry rosato (Teroldego Rotaliano)

Serves 4-6; Preparation: 30 minutes+1 hour to soak the mussels; Cooking: 30 minutes; Level of difficulty: Medium
Soak the mussels in a large bowl of water for at least an hour to purge them of sand. Pull off their beards, scrub, and rinse well in abundant cold water. § Put the mussels in a large skillet over high heat, sprinkle with the wine, and cover. § When all the shells are open (discard any that don't open), remove from the skillet. Pick the mussels out of their shells one by one. § Bring the water, butter, and salt to a boil in a small pot, add the flour, and remove from the heat. Beat with a wooden spoon until the mixture is thick and well mixed. § Return to medium heat and stir until the mixture sticks to the sides and bottom of the pot. § Let cool. Transfer to a bowl, stir in the eggs one by one, and add the parsley, parmesan, and mussels. § Heat the oil to very hot. Use a spoon to add small quantities of the mussel batter into the oil. The dumplings will swell and turn golden brown. § Drain on paper towels, sprinkle with salt, and serve hot.

Right:
Mousse di tonno

INGREDIENTS

- 12 scallops in shell
- 2 tablespoons finely chopped parsley
- 1 clove garlic, finely chopped
- 3 tablespoons extra-virgin olive oil
- salt and freshly ground black pepper
- juice of 1 lemon

*Wine: a dry rosato
(Teroldego Rotaliano)*

CAPE SANTE ALLA VENETA
Scallops Venetian-style

Serves 4; Preparation: 10 minutes; Cooking: 10 minutes; Level of difficulty: Simple

Pry open the shells, take out the scallops, and rinse under cold running water. § Sauté the parsley and garlic with the scallops in the oil. Season with salt and pepper. § Cook for 4-5 minutes over high heat, stirring continuously. Remove from the heat and add the lemon juice. § Arrange in four shells and serve.

Cape sante con funghi e besciamella
Scallops with mushrooms and béchamel sauce

Serves 4; Preparation: 15 minutes; Cooking: 40 minutes; Level of difficulty: Medium

Wash the scallops well in cold running water. § Cook over high heat in a skillet until they open. § Remove the meat and simmer for 15-20 minutes in a pot of boiling water. § Boil the shells in a pot of boiling water for a few minutes. Let cool and clean thoroughly. Set aside. § Trim the mushrooms, wash carefully, and pat dry with paper towels. Chop coarsely. § Sauté the onion and garlic in ¼ cup butter. Add the thyme, ham, and mushrooms. Season with salt and pepper and cook for 10 minutes. § Prepare the béchamel sauce. § Use the remaining butter to grease the shells. § Chop the scallop meat coarsely and fill the shells. § Stir the mushroom mixture into the béchamel sauce and spoon over the scallops. § Sprinkle with the parmesan and place on a baking sheet in a preheated oven at 400°F for 10-15 minutes. § Serve hot.

Torta di gamberi
Shrimp pie

Serves 6; Preparation: 30 minutes; Cooking: 50 minutes; Level of difficulty: Simple

§ Shell the shrimp and remove the dark intestinal veins. Chop off the heads, and rinse thoroughly in cold running water. § Sauté over medium-high heat for 5 minutes in a skillet with the garlic and butter. § Pour in the brandy and cook for 2 minutes more, stirring all the time. Season with salt and pepper and remove from the heat. § Roll out the pastry dough very thinly and line an ovenproof pie dish 8-9 inches in diameter. § In a bowl combine the eggs, flour, salt and pepper, and mix until smooth. § Add the parsley, cream, shrimp, and the liquid they produced while cooking. Pour into the pie dish and bake in a preheated oven at 400°F for 40 minutes. § Serve hot or at room temperature.

■ INGREDIENTS

- 8 fresh scallops
- 10 ounces white mushrooms
- 1 small onion, finely chopped
- 1 clove garlic, finely chopped
- ⅓ cup butter
- ½ tablespoon finely chopped fresh thyme
- 2 ounces chopped ham
- salt and freshly ground black pepper
- 1 quantity béchamel sauce (see recipe p. 20)
- 4 tablespoons freshly grated parmesan cheese

Wine: a dry white
(Tocai di Lison)

■ INGREDIENTS

- 1½ pounds shrimp
- 2 cloves garlic, finely chopped
- 3 tablespoons butter
- 2 tablespoons brandy
- salt and freshly ground black pepper
- 14 ounces plain pastry (store-bought)
- 3 eggs
- 2 tablespoons all-purpose flour
- 4 tablespoons finely chopped parsley
- 6½ ounces fresh cream

Right:
Cape sante con funghi e besciamella

ARINGHE FRESCHE MARINATE
Marinated herrings

Serves 6-8; Preparation: 30 minutes + 24 hours; Cooking: 40 minutes; Level of difficulty: Medium
Sauté half the carrots, thyme, bay leaves, and peppercorns in a skillet with the butter for 3-4 minutes. § Add the flour and cook for 2-3 minutes more. § Add the wine, vinegar, salt, sugar, parsley, cinnamon, cilantro, and cloves. Bring to a boil and cook over low heat for about 30 minutes, or until the liquid has reduced by about a third. § Remove from the heat and add the marjoram. § Clean the herrings, cut off the heads, wash and pat dry with paper towels. § Arrange the herrings in a single layer in a large pan and pour the hot marinade over the top. Cover and cook over low heat for 10-12 minutes. § When cool, transfer to a large flat dish and cover with the marinade. Keep in a cool place for at least 24 hours. § Remove from the marinade and arrange on a serving dish. Sprinkle with the remaining carrots, the onion, the lemon juice, and a tablespoon or two of marinade.

■ INGREDIENTS
- 4 ounces carrots, very finely sliced
- dash each of thyme, cinnamon, marjoram
- 2 bay leaves
- 10 white peppercorns
- 2 tablespoons butter
- 1 tablespoon all-purpose flour
- 2 cups dry white wine
- 1 cup white wine vinegar
- salt
- 1 tablespoon sugar
- 1 tablespoon finely chopped parsley
- 1 teaspoon cilantro
- 4 cloves
- 12 fresh herrings
- 1 small onion, finely chopped
- juice of 1 lemon

Wine: a dry rosato (Salice Salentino)

POMPELMI RIPIENI
Grapefruit filled with shrimp

Serves 4; Preparation: 20 minutes + 30 minutes in the refrigerator; Cooking: 10 minutes; Level of difficulty: Simple
Cut the grapefruit in half and with a sharp knife extract the pulp. Take care not to cut or spoil the grapefruit shells which are used to serve the shrimp. Remove the white membrane and dice the pulp (in a dish or plate so that the juice is conserved). § Put the onion, celery, bay leaves, and shrimp in a small pot of cold water and simmer over medium heat for about 10 minutes, or until the shrimp are cooked. § Prepare the mayonnaise and combine with the mustard. Mix well and stir in the lemon and grapefruit juice. § Remove the shells from the shrimp and cut off the heads. Chop coarsely and add to the mayonnaise sauce. Stir in the diced grapefruit and fill the grapefruit cups with the mixture. § Place in the refrigerator for about 30 minutes before serving.

■ INGREDIENTS
- 2 grapefruit
- 1 small onion
- 1 stalk celery
- 2 bay leaves
- 1 pound shrimp
- salt
- 1 quantity mayonnaise (see recipe p. 16)
- 2 teaspoons mild mustard
- juice of 1 lemon

Wine: a dry white (Torgiano Bianco)

VARIATIONS
– Sprinkle 2 tablespoons of *bottarga* (roe of tuna fish or gray mullet) over the grapefruit just before serving.
– Spread 1 small can of caviar over the grapefruit just before serving.

Right:
Pompelmi ripieni

Coppini di limoni al tonno
Tuna-fish lemon cups

■ INGREDIENTS

- 4 lemons
- 7 ounces tuna fish in olive oil
- 2 tablespoons capers
- 2 tablespoons pickles
- 2 hard-cooked egg yolks
- extra-virgin olive oil
- 1 quantity mayonnaise (see recipe p. 16)
- salt
- a few lettuce leaves, olives, slices of gherkin and bell peppers, to garnish

Wine: a dry white (Locorotondo)

Serves 4; Preparation: 20 minutes; Level of difficulty: Simple

Cut the lemons in half crosswise. § Using a sharp knife, scoop out the insides without piercing the rind so they can be used as cups. § Put the tuna fish, capers, gherkins, and egg yolks through a food mill several times. § Transfer the mixture to a bowl and add the oil, mayonnaise, and lemon juice. Mix well and fill the lemons. § Arrange on a serving plate on a bed of washed and dried lettuce leaves and garnish with olives and slices of gherkin or bell pepper.

Fritto di calamari e scampi
Fried squid and shrimp

■ INGREDIENTS

- 1 pound small squid
- 8 ounces giant shrimp
- 1 cup all-purpose flour
- 2 cups oil, for frying
- salt
- 1 lemon and 6-8 sprigs parsley, to garnish

Wine: a dry white (Bianco di Pitigliano)

There are one or two golden rules to remember when preparing fried dishes. First, make sure the oil is hot enough before adding the seafood. Check by adding a tiny piece of bread — if it turns golden brown immediately, the oil is ready. Second, don't put too many squid rings or shrimp in the pan at once. If you completely fill the pan, the squid and shrimp will stick together in an unappetizing lump. You will also lower the temperature of the oil too much and the seafood will not seal immediately against the oil and will take longer to cook. This means it will absorb more oil and the dish will be heavier.

Serves 4-6; Preparation: 30 minutes; Cooking: 30 minutes; Level of difficulty: Simple

Clean the squid following the instructions on p. 94. Cut in ¼-inch rings. § Remove the shells and dark intestinal veins from the shrimp, chop off the heads, and rinse thoroughly in cold running water. § Heat the frying oil to very hot in a deep-sided skillet. § Place the flour in a bowl and add the squid rings. Take them out a few at a time, shake off excess flour, and plunge them into the hot oil. Each panful will need about 8 minutes to cook. § Repeat the process with the shrimp, which will take about 5 minutes to cook. § Drain on paper towels to eliminate excess oil, sprinkle with salt, and garnish with slices of lemon and sprigs of parsley. § Serve immediately.

Right:
Coppini di limoni al tonno

■ INGREDIENTS

• 1½ pounds shrimp

• 1¼ cups milk

• 3 eggs

• bunch of chives, finely
  chopped

• salt and freshly ground
  black pepper

• 1 tablespoon butter

Wine: a dry white
(Orvieto Classico)

SFORMATI DI GAMBERI
Shrimp molds

Serves 6; Preparation: 40 minutes; Cooking: 30 minutes; Level of difficulty: Medium

Shell the shrimp and remove the dark intestinal veins. Chop off the heads, and rinse thoroughly in cold running water. Dry well and chop into small pieces. § Combine the milk, eggs, chives, salt and pepper in a bowl and beat with a fork until well mixed. § Add the shrimp and pour the mixture into six 4-inch buttered molds. § Place a large container filled with water in the oven and heat to 350°F. Place the mold pans in the water and cook *bain-marie* for 30 minutes. § Serve warm or cold.

Bruschette di frutti di mare
Seafood bruschette

INGREDIENTS

- 8 ounces mussels in shell
- 8 ounces clams in shell
- 2 tablespoons extra-virgin olive oil
- 2 cloves garlic
- 2 tablespoons finely chopped parsley
- 1 cup dry white wine
- 7 ounces small squid
- 8 ounces shrimp
- 1 red bell pepper
- 1 scallion, finely chopped
- ½ tablespoon butter
- 1 teaspoon saffron, dissolved in ½ cup lukewarm milk
- salt and freshly ground black pepper
- 8 slices bruschetta (see recipe p. 16)

Wine: a dry white (Nosiola)

These bruschette *are easy to make and delicious to eat. Be sure to spoon the seafood sauce over the* bruschette *just before serving. To prepare ahead of time, proceed as far as the thickened sauce and set aside. After an hour or two, reheat the sauce, add the seafood, and finish cooking.*

Serves 4; Preparation: 30 minutes+1 hour to soak; Cooking: 20 minutes; Level of difficulty: Medium

Soak the mussels and clams in a large bowl of cold water for at least an hour to purge them of sand. § Pull the beards off the mussels and scrub both clams and mussels well. Rinse thoroughly under cold running water. Drain well. § Sauté 1 tablespoon olive oil, 1 clove garlic, and 1 tablespoon parsley in a large skillet for 2-3 minutes. § Add the mussels and clams and pour in half the wine. § Cover the pan and place over medium-high heat. Shake the pan often, until the shells are all open. § Drain the liquid they have produced into a bowl, strain and set aside. Discard any shells that haven't opened. § Detach the mussels and clams from their shells and set them aside. § To clean the squid, separate the tentacles and head from the body by grasping the head and pulling it apart from the body. Remove the ink sac from the head. Peel off the skin. Remove the bony part and clean out the insides. Rinse well in cold running water. § Shell the shrimp and remove the dark intestinal veins. Chop off the heads, and rinse thoroughly in cold running water. § Carefully wash the bell pepper, cut in half, remove the seeds and core, and dice. § Sauté the scallion in a skillet with the butter and the remaining oil. Add the diced bell pepper and sauté briefly, stirring continuously with a wooden spoon. § Add the remaining wine and continue cooking over high heat. § When the wine has evaporated, add the mussel liquid and the saffron dissolved in lukewarm milk. Season with salt and pepper. § Continue cooking over high heat for a few minutes until the sauce is thick. Add the mussels, clams, shrimp, and squid and cook for 3 minutes more, mixing often. § Sprinkle with the remaining parsley. § Prepare the *bruschette.* § Spoon the seafood sauce over the *bruschette* and serve hot.

Right:
Bruschette di frutti di mare

CORNETTI DI SALMONE AFFUMICATO CON INSALATA RUSSA
Smoked salmon cones with potato salad

INGREDIENTS

- 7 ounces potatoes
- 2 ounces carrots
- 2 ounces green beans
- 2 ounces frozen peas
- 1 quantity mayonnaise
  (see recipe p. 16)
- 2 tablespoons extra-virgin
  olive oil
- 2 tablespoons capers
- 2 tablespoons diced
  gherkins
- juice of 1 medium lemon
- salt and freshly ground
  black pepper
- 8 slices smoked salmon
  (about 8 ounces)
- 2 hard-cooked eggs and
  sprigs of parsley, to
  garnish

Wine: a dry white
(Riesling dell'Alto Adige)

Serves 4; Preparation: 40 minutes; Cooking: 20 minutes; Level of difficulty: Simple

Wash and peel the potatoes and dice. Scrape the carrots and dice. Snap ends off the green beans and cut in small pieces. § Put the vegetables in a pot of salted, boiling water and cook over medium heat for 15-20 minutes. § Drain the vegetables and set aside to cool. § Prepare the mayonnaise. § When cold, put the cooked vegetables in a pot with the peas, capers, gherkin, and pepper. Add the mayonnaise, reserving some for garnish, and mix well. § Arrange the slices of smoked salmon on a serving platter and put a spoonful of potato salad on the center of each slice. § Roll the salmon up around the salad into a cone. § Garnish the plate with the remaining mayonnaise, sliced hard-cooked eggs, and a few sprigs of parsley. § Serve cold.

> VARIATION
> – Cones of prosciutto, or ham, or raw beef (of the type used for *carpaccio*) can also be used instead of the salmon.

INSALATA DI POLPO
Octopus salad

INGREDIENTS

- 2 pounds octopus
- 1 cup white wine vinegar
- 1 carrot
- 1 stalk celery
- 1 small onion
- 1 clove garlic
- 5 sprigs parsley
- salt and black pepper
- 4 tablespoons extra-virgin
  olive oil
- juice of 1 lemon
- ½ teaspoon dried chilies

Wine: a dry white (Cirò bianco)

Serves 6-8; Preparation: 30 minutes + 2 hours to soften; Cooking: 1 hour; Level of difficulty: Medium

Clean the octopus by removing the sac and beak. § Beat with the handle of a large knife to soften the flesh. § Place the octopus in a large pot of cold water with the vinegar, carrot, celery, onion, garlic, parsley, and salt. § Cover and bring to a boil over high heat. Lower the heat and simmer for an hour. § Remove from the heat and leave to cool in the water. This will take at least 2 hours. This cooling process is very important because it makes the octopus meat tender. § Skin the octopus (it will come away easily together with the suckers—a few of the latter can be added to the salad). Cut the sac in rings and the tentacles in small pieces. § Transfer to a serving dish and season with oil, lemon juice, salt, pepper, and chilies. § Toss well and serve.

Right: *Cornetti di salmone affumicato con insalata russa*

Meat Appetizers

When serving a meat-based dish as an appetizer remember that meat is filling. If you are planning to follow it with pasta and a main dish in the traditional Italian manner, keep the quantities to tempting tidbit-size or your guests will spoil their appetites and all your hard work and planning will be wasted.

Salame e fichi freschi
Salame with fresh figs

■ INGREDIENTS
- 10 ounces fresh green or black figs
- 7 ounces salame, thinly sliced

Figs begin to appear in the markets in Italy in June, but it is not until August that local fig trees begin producing these delicious fruit and the markets are flooded with them. At that point Salame e fichi freschi *make regular appearances as appetizers on many Italian tables. The mixture of the sweet flesh of the fruit with the strong salty taste of the salame is perfect at the end of a long summer day.*

Serves 4-6; Preparation: 5 minutes; Level of difficulty: Simple

Wash the figs thoroughly and pat dry with paper towels. § Remove the rind from the salame. § Arrange the figs and salame on a serving dish. If you can get them, use fig leaves to garnish the dish.

Wine: a dry rosé
(Salice Salentino - Five Roses)

Piccoli spiedini alla salsiccia
Mixed sausage, chicken and vegetable skewers

■ INGREDIENTS
- 1 large zucchini
- 1 red or yellow bell pepper
- 12 cherry tomatoes
- 2 Italian pork sausages
- 1 large chicken breast
- 2 tablespoons mixed finely chopped sage, rosemary, and parsley
- salt and freshly ground black pepper
- 2 tablespoons extra-virgin olive oil

Serves 4; Preparation: 20 minutes + 1 hour to marinate; Cooking: 15 minutes; Level of difficulty: Simple

Wash and dry the zucchini. Trim the ends and chop into ½-inch thick wheels. § Wash and dry the bell pepper. Remove the seeds and cores and chop in squares. § Wash the tomatoes and leave them whole. § Chop the sausages into 1-inch thick slices. § Chop the chicken into squares of about the same size. § Combine all the ingredients in a bowl with the sage, rosemary, parsley, salt, pepper, and oil and leave to marinate in the refrigerator for 1 hour. § Prepare the skewers, alternating pieces of chicken, sausage, and vegetables. § Heat the grill pan to very hot. Place the skewers in it and cook for 10-15 minutes, or until the meat and vegetables are well-cooked. § Serve hot.

Wine: a dry red (Chianti Ruffino)

Right: *Salame e fichi freschi*

Fagottini di prosciutto dolce ai funghi porcini
Prosciutto rolls filled with porcini mushrooms and fontina cheese

If you can't get fresh porcini mushrooms, use white mushrooms in their place. Serve the rolls straight away; they are particularly tasty while still warm.

Serves 4; Preparation: 20 minutes; Cooking: 15 minutes; Level of difficulty: Simple

Wash the mushrooms carefully under cold running water and pat them dry with paper towels. § Separate the stems and caps and dice them into bite-size pieces. § Sauté the stems in the oil with the garlic, calamint (or thyme), and salt and pepper for about 8-10 minutes. Add a little stock to keep the mixture moist. § Add the caps and cook for 5 minutes more, or until the mushrooms are cooked. § Add the cheese, turn off the heat immediately, and mix well. § Distribute the mixture evenly among the slices of prosciutto, placing it in the middle of each. § Fold the ends of the prosciutto around the mixture and tuck them under the package. Tie each with a chive. § Serve immediately.

■ INGREDIENTS

- 7 ounces porcini mushrooms
- 2 tablespoons extra-virgin olive oil
- 1 clove garlic, finely chopped
- 1 tablespoon finely chopped calamint (or thyme)
- salt and freshly ground black pepper
- ½ cup meat stock, made with boiling water and bouillon cube
- ¾ cup fontina cheese
- 8 ounces prosciutto
- 8 long chives

Wine: a dry red (Colli Piacentini)

Involtini di bresaola
Bresaola rolls filled with robiola cheese

Serves 6-8; Preparation: 20 minutes; Level of difficulty: Simple

Wash and dry the arugula and chop finely. § Combine in a bowl with the robiola, salt and pepper, and mix well. § Arrange on the slices of bresaola and roll them up. § Drizzle with the oil, sprinkle with pepper and serve.

■ INGREDIENTS

- 1 bunch arugula (rocket)
- 7 ounces robiola or other soft, creamy cheese
- salt and freshly ground black pepper
- 7 ounces bresaola
- 2 tablespoons extra-virgin olive oil

Wine: a dry red (Carmignano)

Prosciutto e melone
Prosciutto and canteloupe

Be sure to choose the highest quality Parma prosciutto and the sweetest canteloupe. This dish is best in summer since its outcome depends on the canteloupe being exquisitely fresh.

Serves 4; Preparation: 5 minutes; Level of difficulty: Simple

Wash the canteloupe thoroughly under cold running water and slice into pieces measuring about 1-1½ inches wide. § Arrange on a serving dish with the ham and serve.

■ INGREDIENTS

- 10 ounces prosciutto, thinly sliced
- 1 canteloupe, weighing about 1 pound

Wine: a dry rosé (Leverano)

Right: *Prosciutto e melone*

■ INGREDIENTS

- 7 ounces gorgonzola
  cheese
- 4 ounces mascarpone
  cheese
- 1¼ cups finely chopped
  walnuts + some whole
  to garnish
- salt
- 12 ounces ham, cut in 8
  thick slices

Wine: a dry red (Gattinara)

CANNOLI DI PROSCIUTTO COTTO E GORGONZOLA
Ham rolls filled with gorgonzola cheese and walnuts

Serves 4; Preparation: 15 minutes; Level of difficulty: Simple

Combine the gorgonzola, mascarpone, walnuts, and a dash of salt in a bowl and mix to a thick cream. § Spread the mixture on the slices of ham and roll them up. § Chop each roll in half. § Arrange on a serving dish. The rolls will look more attractive if served on a bed of fresh salad leaves (whatever you have on hand) and garnished with a few whole walnuts. § Serve cold.

CROSTINI TOSCANI
Tuscan-style liver crostini

■ INGREDIENTS

- 3 chicken livers
- ½ onion, finely chopped
- 2 tablespoons extra-virgin olive oil
- 1 bay leaf
- ½ glass dry white wine
- ½ small glass dry Marsala
- 5 ounces veal spleen
- 1 tablespoon capers
- 4 anchovy fillets
- salt and freshly ground black pepper
- ½ cup meat stock, made with boiling water and bouillon cube
- scant 1 cup light cream
- scant ½ cup butter
- 4-8 slices bread

Wine: a dry red
(Brunello di Montalcino)

Serves 4; Preparation: 15 minutes; Cooking: 50 minutes; Level of difficulty: Medium

Remove the bile and the larger fibres from the chicken livers. Chop coarsely. § Sauté the onion over medium heat with the oil. Add the bay leaf and chicken liver. § Brown the chicken liver for 5 minutes, then add the wine and Marsala. § Remove the skin from the spleen and chop coarsely. § As soon as the liquid has completely evaporated, add the spleen to the skillet together with the capers and anchovies. § Season with salt and pepper and cook for 40 minutes. Add a little hot stock whenever the mixture starts to dry out. § Remove from the heat, discard the bay leaf, and put the mixture through a food mill. § Place the mixture in a heavy-bottomed pan over low heat and stir in the cream and half the butter. Stir continuously until it begins to bubble, then remove from the heat. § Cut the bread in slices or triangles and spread lightly with the remaining butter. Place on a baking sheet and toast lightly in the oven. § Spread with the liver mixture, arrange on a serving dish, and serve.

CROSTINI RUSTICI
Country-style liver crostini

■ INGREDIENTS

- 1 stalk celery
- 1 carrot
- 1 onion
- 1 clove garlic
- 1 tablespoon finely chopped parsley
- 4 tablespoons extra-virgin olive oil
- 3 chicken livers
- ½ glass dry white wine
- 3 tablespoons coarsely chopped capers
- 2 anchovy fillets, chopped
- salt and black pepper

Serves 4; Preparation: 15 minutes; Cooking: 30 minutes; Level of difficulty: Medium

Chop the celery, carrot, onion, and garlic together coarsely. § Add the parsley and sauté in a skillet with the oil over medium heat. § Remove the bile and the larger fibres from the chicken livers. Chop coarsely. § Add the chicken livers to the skillet and sauté for 4-5 minutes. § Add the wine and continue cooking over low heat for 20 minutes. If the mixture drys out too much during cooking add a little stock made with boiling water and bouillon cube. § Add the capers and cook for 2-3 minutes. § Add the anchovies and season with salt and pepper. Remove from the heat. § Toast the bread until light gold. Spread with the liver mixture and serve.

Right: Crostini toscani

Insalata di pollo e mandorle
Chicken and almond salad

■ INGREDIENTS

- 1 boiled chicken
- 1 cup shelled almonds
- 2 avocados
- juice of 1 lemon
- 1 lettuce heart
- salt and freshly ground black pepper
- 2 quantities mayonnaise (see recipe p. 16)
- 2 carrots, finely chopped
- 1 celery heart, finely chopped
- 2 tablespoons finely chopped parsley

Wine: a dry white
(Frascati)

Serves 4-6; Preparation: 20 minutes + 2 hours in the refrigerator; Level of difficulty: Simple
Remove the skin from the chicken and discard sinews and bones. § Cut the meat into small pieces. § Blanch the almonds for 2-3 minutes in boiling water and peel. § Peel the avocados. Chop into cubes and sprinkle with lemon juice so they won't turn black. § Line a salad bowl with the best leaves from the heart of the lettuce. § Arrange the chicken in the center and cover with the avocado and almonds. Season with salt and pepper. § Set aside in the refrigerator for at least 2 hours. § Prepare the mayonnaise. § Add the carrots, celery, and parsley to the mayonnaise. § Just before serving, pour half the mayonnaise over the chicken and mix carefully. Serve the rest of the mayonnaise separately at table.

Insalata di pollo e sedano
Chicken and celery salad

■ INGREDIENTS

- 1 boiled chicken
- 1 celery heart
- 5 gherkins
- 4 ounces gruyère cheese
- 4 ounces ham, in one thick slice
- juice of 1 lemon
- salt and freshly ground black pepper
- 1 quantity mayonnaise (see recipe p. 16)

Wine: a dry white
(Pinot Grigio)

Serves 4-6; Preparation: 15 minutes + 30 minutes in the refrigerator; Level of difficulty: Simple
Remove the skin from the chicken and discard sinews and bones. § Cut the meat into small pieces. § Wash the celery and chop coarsely. § Slice the gherkins and dice the gruyère and ham. § Combine the ingredients in a deep salad bowl and season with lemon juice, salt and pepper. § Prepare the mayonnaise and pour over the salad. Toss carefully. § Set aside in the refrigerator for 30 minutes before serving.

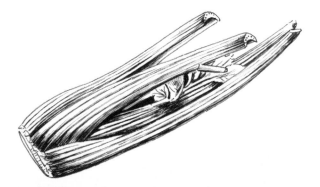

Left
Insalata di pollo e mandorle

Pâté lombardo
Lombard-style pâté

■ INGREDIENTS

• 5 chicken livers
• 1 pound calf's liver, coarsely chopped
• ¼ cup butter
• 1 clove garlic, finely chopped
• 2 tablespoons finely chopped parsley + sprigs to garnish
• salt and freshly ground black pepper
• 1 cup Marsala
• 1½ cups bread crumbs
• 2 eggs + 2 yolks
• 1 cup freshly grated parmesan cheese

Wine: a dry red (Oltrepò Pavese)

Serves 6; Preparation: 25 minutes; Cooking: 40 minutes; Level of difficulty: Medium

Remove the bile and the larger fibres from the chicken livers and chop coarsely. § Sauté the chicken and calf's liver together in the butter with the garlic and parsley for a few minutes. Season with salt and pepper. § When the liver starts to dry out, add the Marsala and continue cooking for 5-10 minutes, or until the liver is cooked. § Remove the liver and add the bread crumbs to the juices in the pan. Mix well and remove from the heat. § Put liver and breadcrumbs through a food mill. § Combine the eggs and yolks, liver, bread crumbs, and parmesan in a bowl and mix to obtain a fairly stiff mixture. If it is too dry or firm, soften with a tablespoon or two of stock made with boiling water and a bouillon cube. § Butter a medium-sized mold, line with waxed paper, and fill with the mixture. Put the mold in a large pan of boiling water and leave it for at least 30 minutes, so that the pâté will finish cooking *bain-marie*. § Garnish with sprigs of parsley and serve warm or cold with toasted bread and plenty of butter.

Pâté di fegato
Liver pâté

■ INGREDIENTS

• 1 onion, finely chopped
• scant ½ cup butter
• 10 ounces calf's liver
• 1 cup lard
• 1 tablespoon finely chopped parsley and tarragon
• ½ cup all-purpose flour
• 2 eggs
• dash of nutmeg
• salt and freshly ground white pepper

Wine: a dry red (Barolo)

Serves 6; Preparation: 30 minutes; Cooking: 50 minutes; Level of difficulty: Medium

Sauté the onion in 1 tablespoon of butter over medium heat. § When it begins to turn golden, turn off the heat and add the remaining butter so it will melt without bubbling. § Cut the liver and lard in small pieces and put through a meat grinder, using the disk with small holes. § Transfer the mixture to a large bowl and add the onion, parsley, and tarragon. § Chop finely in a food processor. § Add the flour, eggs, nutmeg, salt and pepper, and mix thoroughly. § Butter a medium-sized mold, line with waxed paper, and fill with the mixture. Shake the mold to fill up any air pockets. § Cover with a sheet of waxed paper. Fill a large container with boiling water, place the mold in it and cook *bain-marie* in a preheated oven at 350°F for about 45 minutes. § Invert the pâté on a serving dish. § Serve cold.

Right:
Pâté lombardo

Carpaccio di manzo
Raw veal with arugula and artichokes

Serves 6; Preparation: 30 minutes; Level of difficulty: Simple

Trim the artichoke stem, discard the tough outer leaves and trim off the tops. Slice the heart thinly and place in a bowl of cold water with the lemon juice for 10 minutes. § Place the veal in a serving dish. § Beat the oil, wine, capers, salt and pepper together in a bowl until well-mixed. Pour over the veal. § Cover with the arugula, artichokes, and parmesan. § Set aside for 10 minutes before serving.

VARIATIONS
— Replace the arugula and artichoke with 1¼ cups finely chopped white mushrooms. Sprinkle over the meat with the parmesan. Omit the dressing in the recipe above and season with 4 tablespoons extra-virgin olive oil, salt and pepper.
— Omit the dressing, arugula, and artichoke, and replace with flakes of white truffles. Sprinkle over the meat with the parmesan and dress with 4 tablespoons extra-virgin olive oil, salt and pepper.

■ INGREDIENTS

• 1 fresh globe artichoke
• juice of 1 lemon
• 1½ pounds tender, fresh veal, very finely sliced
• ⅓ cup extra-virgin olive oil
• ⅓ cup dry white wine
• 2 tablespoons capers
• salt and freshly ground black pepper
• bunch of arugula (rocket)
• 1 cup parmesan cheese, flaked

Wine: a dry white (Roero Arnesi)

Fesa di tacchino speziata
Spicy turkey meat

Serves 6; Preparation: 30 minutes; Cooking: 40 minutes; Level of difficulty: Simple

Season the turkey with salt, pepper, herbs, spices, and 1 tablespoon of oil. Roast in a preheated oven at 400°F for about 40 minutes. Set aside to cool. § Cut in thin slices when cool and arrange on a serving dish. § Combine the garlic, olives, salt, pepper, remaining oil, and chilies in a bowl and mix well. Pour over the turkey meat. § Sprinkle with the marjoram and serve.

■ INGREDIENTS

• 1¼ pounds turkey meat (from drumsticks)
• salt and freshly ground mixed pepper
• 1 tablespoon finely chopped marjoram
• 1 teaspoon freshly ground juniper berries
• 1 teaspoon freshly ground cilantro seeds
• 1 clove garlic, finely chopped
• 1 cup pitted and chopped green olives
• 2 tablespoons extra-virgin olive oil
• ½ teaspoon crushed chilies

Wine: a dry red (Dolcetto)

Right: Carpaccio di manzo

Index

Gorgonzola cheese
~ Toppings for polenta
  crostini 18
Grapefruit
~ Grapefruit filled with
  shrimp 102
Green beans
~ Green bean mold 54
Green olives 12
Grilled zucchini with fresh
  mint and garlic 30
Gruyère cheese 11
~ Cheese tortelli 82
~ Crêpes with four-cheese
  filling 74
~ Saffron cheese pie 82

Ham 10
~ Ham and cheese
  tidbits 84
~ Ham rolls filled with
  gorgonzola cheese and
  walnuts 115
Hard-cooked eggs with bell
  pepper sauce 60
Herbs and spices 8
Herrings
~ Marinated herrings 102
Hot and spicy green olives
  26

Lemon
~ Carrot salad with garlic,
  oil, and lemon 28
~ Tuna-fish lemon cups 104
Little pizzas with tomato,
  onion, and mozzarella
  cheese 70
Liver
~ Liver pâté 120
~ Toppings for polenta
  crostini 18

Lollo rosso
~ Rainbow salad 43
Lombard-style pâté 120

Marinated zucchini with
  spicy mayonnaise 30
Marinated herrings 102
Marjoram 8
Mascarpone 11
~ *Bruschetta* with spring
  carrots and mascarpone
  cheese 65
~ Cheese and walnut
  mousse 63
~ Tuna-fish mousse 98
Mayonnaise 16
~ *Barchette* with herb
  mayonnaise and truffles 55
~ Marinated zucchini with
  spicy mayonnaise 30
~ Omelet roll 78
~ Scallop shells filled with
  fish, potato, and
  mayonnaise 96
~ Smoked salmon cones
  with Russian salad 108
Meat sauce 22
~ Semolina molds 80
Mint 9
~ Grilled zucchini with
  fresh mint and garlic 30
~ Mint omelet 80
Mixed baked vegetables 52
Mixed sausage, chicken, and
  vegetable skewers 112
Mortadella 10
Mozzarella cheese 11
~ Artichokes with mozzarella 50
~ Cheese-filled *barchette* 85
~ Fried mozzarella 87
~ Fried mozzarella and
  polenta cubes 76
~ Fried polenta with
  mushroom, peas, and
  cheese 48

Mozzarella cheese
~ Little pizzas with tomato,
  onion and mozzarella
  cheese 70
~ Mozzarella and mixed
  pickled vegetables 87
~ Mozzarella and tomato
  slices with fresh vegetables
  45
~ Mozzarella *crostini* Puglia-
  style 75
Muscatel raisins
~ Filled sweet squid 94
Mushrooms
~ Caesar's mushrooms salad 32
~ *Crostoni* with eggs and
  mushrooms 32
~ Filled mushroom caps 52
~ Fried polenta with
  mushroom, peas and
  cheese 48
~ Mushrooms with bay leaf,
  cinnamon, and garlic 44
~ Scallops with mushrooms
  and béchamel sauce 100
~ Tasty braised mushrooms 33
Mussels 13
~ Baked mussels 92
~ Mussel dumplings 98
~ Mussels in pepper sauce 90
~ Seafood *bruschette* 106
~ Seafood salad 96
~ Stuffed baked mussels 90

Nutmeg 9

Octopus 13
~ Octopus salad 108
Olives
~ Hot and spicy green olives
  26
~ Spicy turkey meat 122
~ Stuffed olives 46
Omelet roll 78

Onion
~ Cucumber and onion
   salad 39
~ Little pizzas with tomato,
   onion and mozzarella
   cheese 70
Onion
~ Stuffed onions 57
~ Tuscan bread salad 43
Orange
~ *Crostoni* with asparagus
   and orange sauce 38
Oregano 9

P aprika 8
Parmesan cheese
   (parmigiano) 11
~ Bell peppers filled with
   parmesan and ricotta 64
~ Cheese tortelli 82
~ Crêpes with four-cheese
   filling 74
~ Crostini with four cheeses 60
~ Fried parmesan puffs 74
~ Parmesan and spinach
   dumplings 76
~ Parmesan puffs 70
~ Zucchini and parmesan
   pie 78
Pear
~ Cheese and walnut
   mousse 63
~ Fried polenta with
   mushroom, peas, and
   cheese 48
~ Pear and bell pepper salad
   40
~ Pears with gorgonzola
   dolce 63
~ Pecorino cheese, pear and
   walnut salad 67
Pecorino cheese 11
~ Baby zucchini with
   pecorino cheese 63

Pecorino cheese
~ Pecorino cheese, pear, and
   walnut salad 67
Pepper
~ Mussels in pepper sauce 90
~ Pear and pepper salad 40
Peppercorns
~ Tasty braised mushrooms 33
Pine nuts 12
Platter of stuffed vegetables 34
Polenta
~ Fried mozzarella and
   polenta cubes 76
~ Fried polenta pieces with
   porcini mushroom sauce 48
~ Fried polenta with
   mushroom, peas, and
   cheese 48
~ Polenta *crostini* 18
~ Toppings for polenta
   crostini 18
Porcini mushrooms 12
~ Fried polenta pieces with
   porcini mushroom sauce 48
~ Porcini mushroom salad 44
~ Prosciutto rolls filled with
   porcini mushrooms and
   fontina cheese 114
Potato
~ Scallop shells filled with
   fish, potato, and
   mayonnaise 96
Prosciutto 10
~ Prosciutto and canteloupe
   114
~ Prosciutto rolls filled with
   porcini mushrooms and
   fontina cheese 114
Provolone 11
~ Egg, provolone, apple,
   and radicchio salad 84
~ Sweet and sour fried
   cheese 81

R adicchio
~ Egg, provolone, apple,
   and radicchio salad 84
Rainbow salad 43
Raisins 12
Raw veal with arugula and
   artichokes 122
Red onion 9
Red, white, green, and black
   peppercorns 9
Rice
~ Rice croquettes 50
Ricotta 11
~ Bell peppers filled with
   parmesan and ricotta 64
~ Celery stalks filled with
   gorgonzola and ricotta 37
~ Ricotta with herbs 68
~ Saffron cheese pie 82
Roasted bell peppers with
   anchovies 28
Robiola
~ Bresaola rolls filled with
   robiola cheese 114
~ Toppings for polenta
   crostini 18
Rosemary 8

S affron 8
~ Saffron cheese pie 82
Sage 9
Salame
~ Salame with fresh figs 112
Salmon 13
Salt cod
~ Salt cod fritters 93
Sausage 10
~ Mixed sausage, chicken,
   and vegetable skewers 112
Scallop 13
~ Scallop shells filled with
   fish, potato, and
   mayonnaise 96
~ Scallops Venetian-style 99

Scallops
~ Scallops with mushrooms
and béchamel sauce 100
Seafood 12
~ Seafood *bruschette* 106
~ Seafood salad 96
Semolina molds 80
Shrimp 13
~ Fried squid and
shrimp 104
~ Grapefruit filled with
shrimp 102
~ Seafood *bruschette* 106
~ Seafood salad 96
~ Shrimp molds 105
~ Shrimp pie 100
~ Skewered grilled
shrimp 94
Sicilian-style *crostini* 49
Skewered grilled shrimp 94
Smoked salmon cones with
Russian salad 108
Spicy turkey meat 122
Spinach
~ Parmesan and spinach
dumplings 76
~ Spinach fritters 54
~ Vegetable omelet Emilia-
Romagna style 40
Squid 13
~ Filled sweet squid 94
~ Fried squid and
shrimp 104
~ Seafood *bruschette* 106
~ Seafood salad 96
Stuffed baked mussels 90
Stuffed olives 46
Stuffed onions 57
Sweet and sour fried
cheese 81
Swiss chard
~ Vegetable omelet Emilia-
Romagna style 40

Tarragon 9
Tasty braised mushrooms 33
Time 8
Toasted bread with garlic,
salt and oil 16
Tomato
~ Baked Neapolitan-style
tomatoes 57
~ Basic tomato sauce 22
~ *Bruschette* with fresh
tomato topping 26
~ Cherry tomatoes filled
with caprino cheese 46
~ Little pizzas with tomato,
onion, and mozzarella
cheese 70
~ Mozzarella and tomato
slices with fresh
vegetables 45
~ Mozzarella *crostini* Puglia-
style 75
~ Sicilian-style *crostini* 49
~ Tomato and basil salad 34
~ Toppings for polenta
crostini 18
~ Tuscan bread salad 43
Toppings for polenta *crostini*
18
Truffles
~ *Barchette* with herb
mayonnaise and truffles 55
Tuna-fish 13
~ Tuna-fish lemon cups 104
~ Tuna-fish mousse 98
Turkey
~ Spicy turkey meat 122
Tuscan bread salad 43
Tuscan-style liver *crostini* 116

Veal
~ Raw veal with arugula
and artichokes 122

Vegetables
~ Mixed baked vegetables 52
~ Mixed sausage, chicken,
and vegetable skewers 112
~ Mozzarella and mixed
pickled vegetables 87
~ Mozzarella and tomato
slices with fresh
vegetables 45
~ Platter of stuffed
vegetables 34
~ Vegetable omelet Emilia-
Romagna style 40

Walnuts 12
~ Caesar's mushrooms
salad 32
~ Cheese and walnut
mousse 63
~ Ham rolls filled with
gorgonzola cheese and
walnuts 115
~ Pecorino cheese, pear, and
walnut salad 67
White beans
~ *Bruschetta* with white beans
27
White mushrooms 12
White onion 9
Winter salad 38
– Scallops with mushrooms
and béchamel sauce 100

Zucchini
~ Baby zucchini with
pecorino cheese 63
~ Zucchini and parmesan
pie 78
~ Grilled zucchini with
fresh mint and garlic 30
~ Marinated zucchini with
spicy mayonnaise 30